Journey to Mount Eternity

"I'm sorry that I can't come to dinner tomorrow night," Melissa told Dobson when he came to the phone. "I've decided to go to Mount Eternity after all."

Her words hung in the telephone circuits for a few moments before Dobson spoke. His tone was slow and deliberate.

"You'll never make it Melissa," he predicted. "You'll be back before nightfall. In fact, I'm going to go ahead and have a place set for you at the table."

"You're awfully sure that I'm going to fail, Dobson," Melissa countered.

Dobson laughed, a short, barking sound. "I'll lay odds on it."

As Melissa slammed down the receiver, she could still hear the echo of his mocking laughter.

Books by the same author

Youth Wave Series
Ride the Wave
Wheelin' It

Others
Caught in the Act
Cave of the Living Skeleton
Curse of the Blood Swamp
Danger Down Under
The Forever Friends Club Series
Ghosts at Four O'clock
Hawaiian Summer
Just Between Sisters
Nothing in Common
The Popularity Secret
Project Makeover

Journey to Mount Eternity

Cindy Savage

Illustrated by Maureen Dailey

ONEWORLD
OXFORD

Journey to Mount Eternity

Oneworld Publications
(Sales and Editorial)
185 Banbury Road
Oxford OX2 7AR
England

© Text Cindy Savage 1995
© Illustrations Maureen Dailey 1995
All Rights Reserved
Copyright under Berne Convention

A CIP record for this book is available
from the British Library

ISBN 1–85168–091–8

Printed and bound in Finland by WSOY

Cindy loves to hear from her readers. You may write to her at
P O Box 542, Elk Grove, CA 95624–0542, USA.

The physical journey to Mount Eternity is based on the spiritual journey described by Bahá'u'lláh in *The Seven Valleys*. All italicized sections of the text are quotations from the writings of Bahá'u'lláh, with the exception of the prayers on pages 119 and 132 which are from the writings of 'Abdu'l-Bahá.

Author's Dedication

To my wonderful husband and children.
How blessed I am.

Illustrator's Dedication

To my beloved mother, and to my beloved father, who set
out this year on his own eternal journey.

CHAPTER 1

"Can you believe this?" Melissa Davenport asked her boyfriend, Dobson Wainwright. She pointed to the entry in the Westridge High Senior Class Yearbook. "They voted us most likely couple to get married and succeed in life with fabulous careers. I mean, everyone else gets comments like, 'most likely to fall down a well,' or 'most likely to kiss a frog,' and we end up with 'married and successful.'"

Dobson laughed. "So, what's the problem? I suppose you think that married and successful is boring?"

Melissa sighed and wondered if this discussion was going to turn into another argument. Lately she and Dobson hadn't seen eye to eye on anything. She couldn't blame him. He hadn't changed. But something was going on inside Melissa that she couldn't explain. The trouble was simple, and incredibly complex at the same time. She was beginning to question everything that she had believed in all of her life up until this moment. Not only that, she was beginning to wonder whether all of the plans that she and Dobson had made for their life together after graduation were really what she wanted to do.

"Yes, as a matter of fact, I *do* think it's boring,"

Melissa finally said. "School is kind of like a job. I've been working at being a student for thirteen years. Now, everyone expects me to go to college, get a job, settle down, have 2.2 children and join the country club. What happened to adventure? What happened to spreading our wings and experiencing life from a different angle? Don't you ever wonder what it would be like to break out of the mold?"

"Not really," Dobson said, shaking his head. "I *like* the mold. I'm looking forward to going to college, then law school, and joining my father's law firm just like my brother did. Then I'm going to save up my money and buy a yacht. There's plenty of adventure sailing on the high seas!"

"I guess," Melissa remarked, but she wasn't convinced. Privately she thought that Dobson would probably spend more time entertaining in the yacht club lounge than sailing out of the harbor. And, as his wife, she would be expected to act the part of the lawyer's wife. Oh, she'd have her own career, but her main job would be the role of hostess and ornament. She wasn't sure she was ready to become her mother.

"I'd just like to explore more possibilities before I settle on a plan for my whole life," she added.

"Well, listen, Miss Philosophical, I have to get to class. I'll see you after school. Maybe you'll be done thinking your heavy thoughts by then and we can go out and celebrate the first night of spring vacation!"

"Sounds like fun," Melissa mumbled automatically. But as Dobson had remarked, her thoughts weren't on the night ahead or the week of parties and outings that her friends had planned for vacation. Her thoughts were on her mother.

She opened the door to her fifth period study hall and took her seat in the back of the room. She opened her trigonometry book, but the equations blurred before her eyes. Instead she replayed the discussion she'd had with her mother the evening before.

"I don't know, Mom," Melissa had said. "It feels like something is missing in my life. I know I shouldn't feel that way. I have a comfortable home, great parents, get good grades . . . "

"Don't forget those trophies in track," her mother had added.

"That, too," Melissa had agreed. "And I'm saving money for college by doing a few modeling jobs. I'm really lucky, but . . . "

"But something is missing," her mother had completed, smiling. "Maybe it's your potential. Maybe you're yearning for all of the possibilities the future might hold. It's almost the end of your senior year. It's natural that you're getting tired of school and ready to pursue your dreams."

"But what are my dreams, Mom? I don't even know. I haven't picked a major in college. I'm not even sure that I want to go to Tufts University."

Mrs. Davenport's face was filled with concern. "Is this about Dobson? I thought you wanted to go to the same college? You're already accepted and everything. Is something wrong between you two?" she asked worriedly.

Melissa couldn't meet her eyes. She knew that her parents approved of the match between Dobson, the heir to the Wainwright shipping fortune, and herself, the only child of Dick Davenport, owner of Davenport Imports. The two families had been close, both socially and in business, for generations.

Her father would have laughed at her uncertainty. How many times had she heard him say, "Melissa, money is the way to happiness. If you have it, you're happy. If you don't, you wish you did. Look at me, I'm happy as a clam."

Melissa hadn't realized that her mind was wandering until her mother interrupted her thoughts. "You can tell me, Melissa. Are you and Dobson having problems?"

"No," Melissa answered, coughing suddenly. "Dobson and I are doing fine. He just seems to have his whole life, and mine, planned out, and I guess I'm feeling a little unorganized and unsure."

Mrs. Davenport smoothed Melissa's wavy brunette hair away from her face with a gentle hand. "As you mature, darling, your path will become much more clear. Your dreams will all be realized when you have a family and watch them grow, when you stand by your husband and help him achieve his dreams, too. Then you'll find the contentment that you're missing now. It's only a matter of time."

Melissa shook her head and dispelled the image of her mother's face. She stared at her trigonometry book until she brought the words and symbols back into focus. "Time," she whispered, closing the book and opening her science text. If all she needed was time to accept the inevitable, then why was she so restless? Why did she worry that having a wonderful husband, job, money and family wouldn't be enough?

She glanced over at the table next to her, at the other students who shared her study hall. They had sat in the same classroom for the entire year and she didn't even know some of their names.

One girl, however, intrigued her: Katherine

Sherwood. Melissa watched her now. Katherine's honey-blond hair draped over the book she was reading, seemingly oblivious to the rest of the world.

It was that whole-hearted attention to her work that interested Melissa. Usually most of the other kids in study hall did anything besides work. They passed notes, fixed their hair, painted their nails or doodled on the covers of their notebooks. But Katherine was always focused on something.

Katherine's ability to stay focused on her studies didn't make her dull, though, Melissa noted. She had observed Katherine at other times in animated conversation with friends, or giving her all at a pep rally for the football team. No, Katherine Sherwood wasn't dull, but she wasn't the same as everyone else either.

The one thing that stood out the most about her, Melissa finally decided, was that she didn't belong to just one crowd of kids. Katherine flowed easily into any group and had friends among both the 'popular' and 'unpopular' kids at school. She always had a kind word and a smile for everyone she passed. Melissa wondered what it would be like to have Katherine as a friend.

At that moment, Katherine looked up from her book and smiled at Melissa. Melissa hesitated for only a second, then smiled back. A moment later both girls went back to their reading, but Melissa couldn't concentrate on science. Once again, she was thinking about her future.

The rain began right after lunch. Sheets of ice cold water drenched the hapless students as they scurried from classroom to classroom. Melissa arrived at the gymnasium soaking wet after running all the way across the campus in the downpour.

"How about that?" Mrs. Baker, her P.E. teacher, commented cheerfully. "Showers before *and* after gym class."

There was a rumble of laughter in the locker room as the girls changed into their gym suits – navy blue shorts and red T-shirts with white socks and tennis shoes.

"We'll probably have to do an hour of calisthenics in the gym because of the rain," Roxanne, Melissa's locker partner, remarked.

"Or worse," Melissa said. "What if we have to take one of those fitness tests? You know, like how many sit ups you can do and how many push ups?"

"Yuck," Roxanne said. "Why don't they just cancel P.E. and we'll send out for pizza!"

"Pizza sounds good to me," Melissa agreed.

Across the locker room, Melissa spotted Katherine. She had pulled her long hair back into a neat ponytail. She looked fresh and energetic – ready to take on whatever task lay before them. Melissa glanced at her own dark, straggly hair as she passed the mirror mounted at the end of the row of lockers. She didn't feel ready to face P.E., or anything else, at that particular moment. She wished she knew Katherine's secret for perpetual cheerfulness.

"OK, ladies," Mrs. Baker said as soon as the class was assembled in the gym. "I know you were all looking forward to an hour of exercises or a fitness test . . . "

A chorus of groans filled the room.

"But today we're going to do something different and fun! We're going to play Unity Ball!"

"What's that, Mrs. Baker?" Roxanne asked.

Mrs. Baker stood up and lifted up a huge, air-filled

rubber ball that she had been standing in front of. It was at least four feet in diameter and jiggled like a jellyfish when she held it up.

"This is the Unity Ball," Mrs. Baker announced. "The object of the Unity Ball game is to work as a team. No one wins or loses, but you and your partner, along with the rest of the class, will have to work together in *unity* to achieve your goal."

"Which is?" another girl asked from the other side of the room.

Mrs. Baker smiled. "The goal is to keep the ball in the air . . . "

"That sounds easy enough," Roxanne whispered to Melissa.

" . . . without using your hands!" Mrs. Baker concluded. "*And* you must play the game while walking spider style on your hands and feet. Now, choose partners with whom you may talk and plan your efforts."

"Uh-oh," Melissa said as she dropped down backward on the floor and balanced herself on her arms and legs. "I don't think it's going to be as easy as we thought."

"Fun, though," a voice said from a similar spider position next to her. It was Katherine.

"Oh, hi!" Melissa said.

"Want to be my partner?" Katherine asked.

"Sure," Melissa said, wondering where Katherine had appeared from all of a sudden, since a moment ago she had been all the way across the gym.

Mrs. Baker blew her whistle. "Does everyone have their partners?"

Heads nodded all around the room.

"OK. I'm setting the stopwatch. When I say 'begin,' I want you and your partner, and the group as a whole, to find a way to keep that ball in the air as you pass it from one side of the room to the other. Our goal will be ten passes in ten minutes. Begin!"

Katherine grinned. "Here it comes," she said.

The ball rolled and bounced steadily toward them, a giant, wobbling, gelatinous mass. It looked alive. Shrieks went up from around the room as girls began trying to control the Unity Ball. Well-placed kicks sent it high in the air. Girls used their heads, their stomachs, their feet, their knees, but no matter how hard they tried, the ball had a mind of its own, slipping and sliding and falling on the ground, despite their best efforts. It was bigger than one person alone.

"I have an idea," Katherine said. "Let's get right next to each other so that when the ball comes this way, it won't have any ground to fall on."

"I'm with you," Melissa said. "And, here's our chance. Get ready for impact!"

The Unity Ball flew in its jiggly path right toward Katherine and Melissa, but the girls were braced and ready. It landed with a plop on their upraised stomachs, wobbled for a second, then was still.

Melissa grinned at Katherine. "Well, we've got it. Now what do we do with it?"

"Let's try walking together," Katherine suggested. "Maybe we can take it part way across the room."

Slowly, Melissa and Katherine inched their way across the gymnasium floor, balancing the Unity Ball on the table they had made with their stomachs.

"It's working!" Melissa whispered. "But I'm getting tired. There's no way we'll make it to the other side of the gym. Hey, everybody," she called out to the other girls. "Form a giant table and we'll roll it across the room."

"It'll never have to touch the floor," Katherine added.

Quickly people began to get the idea, lining up as close to each other as possible and making their movements count instead of flailing their legs wildly in the air.

When the ball slowly made its way to the other side of the room for the first time, a cheer went up from the class, and within a few seconds, Melissa saw the ball rolling calmly back in their direction for its second trip.

"I see why they call it Unity Ball," Melissa commented to Katherine as they once again received the ball and, in unison, sent it back the other way with identical heaves of their stomachs.

"I'm having fun!" Katherine said, smiling. "It really makes a difference when everyone works together for a common goal."

"You seemed to understand the spirit of the game immediately," Melissa remarked. "You knew what we had to do. I probably would have been kicking and screaming just like all of the other girls."

"Everyone would have figured it out eventually," Katherine said. "It was only a matter of trial and error . . . and time."

"Time . . . " Melissa mused as she watched the ball flow over the sea of bodies. "I've been thinking a lot about time lately. There's so little time before we graduate, so much time afterward, and I don't have any idea what I want to do with mine."

"I thought you had your life all planned," Katherine said. "I read about you and Dobson in the yearbook."

Melissa laughed, but it wasn't a happy sound. "I know. Everyone else knows what's happening in my life except me. I just don't know if I'm ready to go to college and then settle down permanently with the guy I've been going with for the past two years. I don't know what I want any more. All I know is that I'm confused."

Katherine was quiet, waiting for Melissa to go on.

Suddenly Melissa realized that she had been spilling her most private thoughts to an almost complete stranger. "I'm sorry," she said. "I don't know why I'm even telling you this. You must think I'm crazy."

Katherine's eyes twinkled with warmth as she smiled at Melissa. "Not crazy – normal," she said. "And don't worry. Your secret is safe with me."

Somehow Melissa never doubted that. She knew instinctively that Katherine was an honest, trustworthy person. And she was glad that she had voiced her thoughts aloud.

"I'll bet you know exactly what you're going to do with your life," Melissa said.

Katherine shook her head. "Not all of it," she told her. "But it doesn't really matter what my plans are. Your plans have to be right for you. I used to be really confused, too," she admitted. "But a couple of years ago I went on a special trip. Getting away really helped me put things in perspective."

"Where did you go?" Melissa asked eagerly. "I'd love to get away from my problems right now."

The ball came toward them again and, without a word, the girls got into position and passed it back toward the center.

"As a matter of fact, I'm going on the trip again during spring break next week. A group of us are backpacking up Mount Eternity. Would you like to come along?"

"Mount Eternity?" Melissa exclaimed, impressed. "You've hiked up Mount Eternity before? I've never met anyone who has actually made it to the top."

"Lots of people have made it," Katherine assured her. "Have you done any hiking in the past?"

Melissa nodded. "Quite a bit. And I'm on the track team. But I've never gone on a hike as long and arduous as tackling Mount Eternity." She thought of the snow-capped mountain peak that stood sentinel across the valley from where she had lived all of her life. If she took time to admit it, she had gazed longingly in that direction many times, wondering what it would be like to scale the misty slopes.

"Ten!" Mrs. Baker shouted and blew her whistle, breaking into Melissa's thoughts. "Congratulations, girls. That was the most efficient and unified game of Unity Ball that I've ever seen played. Your reward is being dismissed early. Hit the showers!"

"I meant what I said about you being welcome to come with us on our trip," Katherine said as the two girls strolled into the locker room together. "Coming along might give you a chance to sort out your feelings and goals."

"Your invitation is really tempting," Melissa said. "I'm sure my parents would let me go . . . but my boyfriend would think I was nuts."

Katherine laid her hand on Melissa's shoulder. "Think about coming with us. We're leaving tomorrow afternoon. I'll give you my phone number and you can call me with your decision tonight."

"Thanks," Melissa said, genuinely touched by Katherine's thoughtfulness. "I really appreciate the offer and I'll let you know as soon as I decide."

CHAPTER 2

"I can't believe you're really thinking about going on such a crazy trip!" Dobson exploded in the car on their way home after school. "I mean, you barely know this girl and you're going to head off with her and her loony friends to Mount Eternity? Haven't you ever heard the stories about people who try to climb that blasted mountain? They never come back."

"I've heard the stories," Melissa replied patiently. "But haven't you ever wondered what it would be like to climb it?" She turned her gaze out the window to the mist-shrouded slopes in the distance. "I know that only a few people succeed, but wouldn't it be something to be one of them?"

"I think your head is stuck somewhere in those clouds out there," Dobson said, pointing an irritated finger at the mountain. "And besides, what about all of *my* plans for this spring break? I thought we'd go to the beach one day and sailing on another day. And my parents have invited you over for dinner."

"Those were *your* plans, Dobson," Melissa said patiently. "Not mine."

Dobson arched an arrogant eyebrow. "You didn't object when I told you about them before."

Melissa sighed. "It's not that I objected, exactly. It did kind of upset me that you didn't bother to consult with me before you planned our whole week. But I don't want to fight about whose plans we'll follow. I just thought I'd mention Katherine's invitation to Mount Eternity to see what you thought. I even had visions of us going on the trip together."

Dobson slammed his hand down on the steering wheel. "Together? No way! It's such a stupid idea!"

Obviously! Melissa was silent, thinking about Dobson's words. She didn't know which hurt more – his refusal to go with her, or the way he put her down for even considering the idea. Somehow she had to make him understand what a lure the mountain was for her, and how much she wanted to prove herself against it.

"I'd like you to understand why I'm considering this trip," Melissa began hesitantly. "For a while now, I've been wondering just where I'm going with my life. I don't seem to have as clear a focus on my future as you do, Dobson. The chance to pit myself against Mount Eternity seems like a chance to sort out my feelings and goals. I want to do something important with my life. I'm just not sure what that is yet. Maybe climbing the mountain will help me discover who I am."

"Or help you discover who you're *not*," Dobson jeered. "You may not even survive and where would that leave me?"

Trust Dobson to bring the whole issue around to how it affected him, Melissa thought. He wasn't so much worried about her safety, as concerned about his own selfish needs.

Melissa shook her head as they pulled into her driveway. "Katherine assured me that anyone who truly wants to make it will receive the strength to try."

"That's a bunch of pseudo-religious garbage and you know it!" Dobson spat. "I've seen Katherine Sherwood around school, meditating out in the field with a circle of friends, trying to convince people that there's more to life than fame and fortune. I don't know what she's preaching, but it doesn't impress me."

"Whatever she believes in, it must work," Melissa said thoughtfully. "Katherine has been to the top of Mount Eternity several times and she says it gets easier each time she goes."

"Well, I'll tell you one thing," Dobson said, leaning close as she opened the passenger door. "You'll be sorry if you waste your whole vacation on climbing that stupid mountain."

"I haven't decided yet, and I haven't talked to my parents," Melissa told him.

"Let me know," he said, laughing as he drove off. "Remember, dinner tomorrow at eight."

Dobson's assumption that Melissa would give up her 'stupid' idea only served to fix the thought of taking the trip more firmly in her head. She needed some time alone – time away from school and from her parents, and especially from Dobson. He was becoming more overbearing by the day. He tried to run her life, he made plans without asking her opinion, and he scoffed at her serious doubts about her future. She was beginning to wonder what it had been that attracted her to Dobson in the first place.

With every step she took up the driveway to her house, Melissa's determination grew. She *would* go on the hiking trip to Mount Eternity. She *would* show Dobson that she was made of stronger stuff than he thought she was.

When she reached her front door, she pivoted slowly back toward the east and allowed the lure of the mountain to draw her gaze to its very highest pinnacle. She gasped at the sight that greeted her. No longer covered with misty veils, the snowy peak had burst through the clouds and gleamed in the afternoon sunshine. Melissa could feel the pull of the mountain, could almost hear it calling her.

A sudden flash of sunlight ricocheted off the pure white peak, pouring a shaft of sparkling light across the valley until it bathed her in its radiant glow.

"I'm coming," she whispered to the mountain, her face drenched in the soft, warm light. And then the light was gone, obscured once again by the mist. But Melissa could still feel its warmth, and as she turned to enter her house, she felt her conviction grow. She knew in her heart that she needed to ascend Mount Eternity.

Now all she had to do was convince her parents.

"Hello? I'm home!" she called as she dropped her book bag on the catch-all table in the foyer. Melissa hung her jacket in the hall closet and sniffed the aroma of cinnamon and brown sugar.

"We're in here," Mrs. Davenport called.

Melissa followed her nose to the kitchen where she found her mother and father sitting in the breakfast room with a platter of freshly baked cinnamon rolls between them.

"Come on, have a roll," her father invited as he pulled out the chair next to him.

"What's the occasion?" Melissa asked. "Why are you both home so early?"

"We're celebrating," Mr. Davenport said with a smile.

"That shipment of antique jade figurines just came in from China and I already have several buyers lined up, including the Metropolitan Museum of Fine Arts. We're having a little party this evening to show them off."

"That's great, Dad," Melissa said, not quite as enthusiastically as she probably should have. After all, her father was always making deals like this. He specialized in locating and importing rare and hard-to-find items.

"It's more than great, honey," Mrs. Davenport said. "This jade is so exquisite that the media has decided to cover the sale and transfer of the most beautiful pieces to the museum. Channel 3 will be here tonight to film the unveiling!"

"Television!" Melissa exclaimed, taking a bite of her roll. "I guess I'd better go clean my room."

Mr. Davenport chuckled good-naturedly. "Don't fret, Melissa. It's already done. We hired one of those speedy maid services to come over this afternoon and take care of everything. The whole house is ship-shape from stem to stern."

"Thanks," Melissa said, knowing how important appearances were to her parents. Since they were in such good moods, she decided that this might be the time to broach the subject of the trip with them.

Coincidentally, her mother brought up the subject first. "Have another roll," her mother offered. "You have cause to celebrate, too. A whole week of freedom from school! What are you and Dobson planning to do over the spring break?" she asked.

Melissa cleared her throat. "Well, actually, I had a fantastic offer from another friend that I wanted to discuss with you."

She had both of her parents' attention now. She took a deep breath. "A girlfriend of mine at school invited me on a backpack trip for the week and I'd like to go."

"That sounds like fun," Mr. Davenport said. "Where would you hike to?"

"Mount Eternity. A whole group of us would be going with a guide. It's perfectly safe." Melissa's words spilled out in a rush.

"Mount Eternity!" Mrs. Davenport exclaimed, shaking her head. "I don't know. I know you're an experienced camper and hiker, Melissa, but I've heard some terrible stories about . . ."

"And that's probably all that they are – stories," Melissa interrupted. "Katherine has gone several times and she doesn't look any the worse for wear."

"Katherine?"

"Katherine Sherwood, my friend at school. She's the one who invited me. The group is leaving tomorrow afternoon."

Mr. Davenport sighed. "I don't think it's such a good idea, Melissa. I mean, what if you get hurt? There aren't many roads in or out of that place. I've heard that it's wild and dangerous up there, filled with bogs and hidden pitfalls."

"But we'll have a guide, Dad," Melissa argued. "He's an experienced wilderness tracker. Katherine says he leads all of their trips. Besides," she said, trying another tactic, "just think how impressed all of your friends will be when I make it."

Mrs. Davenport smiled. "That's true, Dick. None of our friends or business associates has ever climbed Mount Eternity that I know of. None of their children has either. It *would* be quite an accomplishment, a feather in

Melissa's cap, so to speak. She could even put it down on job applications later."

Melissa nodded encouragingly. "And I promise to be careful," she added. "You know I wouldn't do anything to put myself in danger."

"We'll let you go on one condition," her father declared. "That you promise to turn back if the going gets too difficult."

Melissa sighed with relief. "I promise, Dad."

"And we want to meet Katherine and the rest of the group," her mother added.

"You can meet them when you drop me off at the starting place tomorrow. Oh, thanks!" she said, jumping up and hugging them both. "I think this is going to be just what I need."

Leaving her parents with puzzled expressions on their faces, Melissa rushed upstairs to her room to begin packing. She was careful not to mess up the pristine neatness of the newly cleaned room. As soon as she was done, she called Katherine to tell her she could come. Then she called Dobson.

"I'm sorry that I can't come to dinner tomorrow night," Melissa told him after they had exchanged greetings. "I've decided to go to Mount Eternity after all. I just wanted to let you know."

Her words hung in the telephone circuits for a few silent moments before Dobson spoke. When he did, it wasn't with the ranting and raving that she expected. His tone was slow and deliberate.

"You'll never make it, Melissa," he predicted. "You'll be back before nightfall. In fact, I'm going to go ahead and have a place set for you at the table."

"You're awfully sure that I'm going to fail, Dobson,"

Melissa commented.

Dobson laughed, a short, barking sound. "I'd lay odds on it," he said. "As soon as you hit that wall of impenetrable mist, you'll turn back. Otherwise you may end up like the other poor souls who get lost in the fog. They never even find their bones," he added ominously.

"Are you *trying* to scare me? We're talking about a mountain, Dobson, not the Bermuda Triangle," Melissa countered, not quite able to stop the shiver that ran along her spine.

"Not at all," Dobson replied lightly. "I'm sure you're scared enough as it is."

"Actually," Melissa said, shaking off her growing fear. "I'm *not* scared. I'm *determined* to make it."

Dobson snorted derisively.

"I'm sorry you feel that way," Melissa said. "I thought I'd call to make one more attempt at communication with you, but I can see that you don't care one whit about my feelings in this matter."

"Oh, I care," Dobson said, his tone sarcastic. "I just don't want to see you make a fool of yourself."

"Of course not!" Melissa snapped. "It might rub off on you! In fact, if you're so worried about your reputation, maybe we should just call off our whole relationship. That way, if I make a fool of myself, you'll be in the clear!"

Dobson laughed again. "You don't have any idea what you're talking about, Melissa. I have to go now," he said. "See you tomorrow night at dinner."

As Melissa slammed down the receiver, she could still hear the echo of his mocking laughter.

CHAPTER 3

Her parents' party to unveil Davenport Imports' newest acquisitions was a success. Important members of the community and the media crowded into their luxurious home, basked in the glow of Davenport hospitality, and partook of the catered buffet of rich food.

And all through the evening, Melissa and her trip to Mount Eternity were discussed as much, if not more, than the jade sculptures. It seemed as if her parents were already getting a lot of social mileage out of her decision to go.

"Yep," she heard her father say as he slapped one of his business associates heartily on the back. "Melissa has the Davenport drive. Nothing is impossible. When we want something, we just go for it."

"Melissa has always been a goal-oriented child," her mother boasted to the wife of one of the museum curators. "I'm sure this will only be the beginning."

Melissa fell into bed wearily that night, but she had trouble falling asleep. Visions of her parents' and Dobson's faces swam before her eyes. Her parents were sure she *would* make the trek and, in turn, make them proud. Dobson was sure she *wouldn't* make the trek, and he wanted to make sure that her failure didn't reflect poorly on him.

But what did *she* want? Her reasons for going seemed vague and uncertain. She wanted to prove something to herself. She wanted to sort out her feelings about her future. She wanted to learn more about her own strengths and weaknesses. She wanted to find the missing pieces to the puzzle of her life.

It was a lot to ask of one little week-long backpack trip.

Melissa was still wondering whether she was being foolish to put so much hope into one week away from home when her parents drove her to the group's meeting place the next afternoon.

But despite her misgivings, she was as curious as they were to meet the other people who would be journeying up Mount Eternity with her.

Katherine came over to the car to greet them. "Welcome!" she said, smiling at Melissa and her parents. "I'm Katherine Sherwood," she offered, shaking hands with the Davenports. "Come on over. I'll introduce you to everyone."

Katherine led the way to the others and said, "These are the Malones, Richard and Mary. Richard and Mary were recently married and this is their honeymoon trip."

"How do you do?" Mr. Davenport asked, extending his hand first to Mary and then to Richard.

"Just fine," Mary replied. "We're looking forward to this trip. I'm sure we'll have a great time."

"We certainly wish you a good journey," Mrs. Davenport said.

"Hi," Melissa said, studying the newly weds. They didn't seem out of the ordinary. Both were fairly young, dark-haired, and had pleasant smiles.

"Nice to meet you," Richard said.

"And this is Elise Donaldson," Katherine told them, indicating a tall, older African-American woman, perhaps in her mid-fifties. She was leaning on a cane.

"Ah, another searching soul," Elise remarked, offering her free hand to Melissa. "I'm really excited about this trip, aren't you?"

Melissa nodded. "Absolutely."

"I just hope you'll all be very careful," Mrs. Davenport cautioned.

"We'll watch out for each other," Elise assured her.

At that moment, a distinguished-looking older gentleman with a white beard approached the circle.

"This is Haddi, our guide," Katherine said, smiling at Haddi and then at the group. She introduced them each in turn.

"I understand you've been on this journey many times," Mr. Davenport began.

"Your daughter's safety is well-assured," Haddi said with a warm smile, seeming to read the unspoken question in Mr. Davenport's comment.

"Thank you," her father said. "I'm sure she's in good hands."

"The best!" Katherine assured him. "Maybe next time you'll make the journey with us?"

Mrs. Davenport laughed softly. "Not me. You won't catch me sleeping on the cold, hard ground. The closest I get to camping is a five-star hotel."

"I'll second that," Mr. Davenport said with a laugh. "But I admire you all for braving the elements. Godspeed!"

After her parents left, Melissa helped Katherine

divide up the community food, pots, pans and utensils. Each person was going to share the task of carrying the supplies.

Though it was still early, Haddi built a fire and put on a pot of water for tea.

"Please join me around the fire," he invited.

"I'm really thrilled to be going on this trip," Mary Malone commented as she sat down next to her husband.

"We're going to have a great time," Richard predicted confidently, smiling at Melissa, Katherine and Elise. "And it will be nice getting to know all of our new friends on the way."

"Since we just moved to Seaside, we don't know many people yet," Mary confided as they all took their seats.

"Well, there's lots to do in Seaside," Katherine assured her. "I'll be happy to give you a tour when we get back."

"And I'll introduce you to my daughter and her husband," Elise added. "They're about your age."

"That would be wonderful," Mary said, smiling happily. "We'll appreciate all the help we can get."

Katherine sat next to Melissa and leaned close to her. "Some of the things Haddi says may sound strange at first, but if you listen and follow the path of your heart, your journey will be much easier."

"Thanks," Melissa said. "I'll do my best."

Once again, Melissa was struck by how kind Katherine was. She had an encouraging word for everyone. She thought fleetingly about Dobson. If he had given her just one word of encouragement, she would have considered it a miracle!

"First, I would like us all to take a moment of silence

to meditate on the journey ahead," Haddi said. He closed his eyes and sat perfectly still. The rest of the members of the group followed his example and Melissa, although surprised, took the opportunity to gather her thoughts one last time before the journey began.

Closing her eyes seemed strange, so instead she found herself staring at the cracking fire, mesmerized by its golden flames. A warm feeling of contentment washed over her, as though everything that she had done in her life so far had brought her to this exact moment, with this exact group of people, sitting around this particular fire. And the journey ahead was something that she knew, with certainty, that she must do. Melissa didn't understand why she suddenly felt so strongly about the days ahead, but she decided not to dwell on the reasons, and concentrate instead on the moment of peace.

A few minutes later, Haddi began reciting, in a low, soft voice, what Melissa took to be a prayer. *"Praise be to God Who hath made being to come forth from nothingness; graven upon the tablet of man the secrets of pre-existence; taught him from the mysteries of divine utterance that which he knew not; made him a Luminous Book unto those who believed and surrendered themselves; caused him to witness the creation of all things in this black and ruinous age, and to speak forth from the apex of eternity with a wondrous voice in the Excellent Temple: to the end that every man may testify, in himself, by himself, in the station of the Manifestation of his Lord, that verily there is no God save Him, and that every man may thereby win his way to the summit of realities, until none shall contemplate anything whatsoever but that he shall see God therein."* He paused for a moment and then added, *"Peace be upon him who followeth the Right Path!"*

Melissa allowed his words to wash over her, but she

didn't understand them. Since they were heading to Mount Eternity, the highest peak of the Summits of Wonderment, she assumed that it was just the guide's eccentric way of wishing them all good luck and Godspeed.

He opened his eyes and looked at each one in turn. "This fire," he began, "though it looks like an ordinary fire, has an eternal, symbolic meaning. It was lit from the Lamp of Pre-Existence. Every fire that has ever been lit, and every fire that will ever be lit in the future, is connected to this fire, just as every soul who has ever made this journey or will ever make this journey is connected to each of you."

"I think I understand," Elise said. "It's like there's an invisible thread, joining everyone to each other, a common bond, so to speak."

"People try to find ways to separate themselves from one another, but it's really fruitless," Katherine remarked. "We're all the same underneath the outward trappings."

"The light that shines from within is the same, no matter the shape or color of the lamp," Haddi explained. "As we start on this journey, we would do well to leave our conceptions of ourselves behind. Whether we are rich or poor, young or old, male or female, black, brown or white, does not matter in the sight of God. Each person has value and must contribute to the best of their ability and, in turn, each will reach the goals they seek when the time is right. On this journey, we are all one."

Melissa was beginning to wonder if their guide and some of her fellow travelers were a little flaky after all. Sure, she had a feeling of peace when she looked into the fire, but to connect that feeling to every person from the dawn of time was a little beyond her imagination. She had her own goals for this trip, and they didn't really have anything to do with pre-existence or post-existence, or whatever Haddi had said. She glanced over at Katherine to see how she was taking all this spiritual mumbo-jumbo. But Katherine was still listening intently to the guide.

"From this moment on," Haddi continued, smiling at Melissa and the others, "no one will be the same. This journey will change you, each of you, in different ways."

He allowed that statement to sink in and everyone was silent for a moment, contemplating the implication of his words as he began to serve the tea.

Melissa felt a shiver of excitement run up her spine as she accepted the cup of tea that he handed out to her. Although only an hour before her parents had driven her to the meadow where they were to begin their journey, it now seemed like a different place. The small group of wayfarers, sipping tea around the fire, seemed very isolated, very removed from the hustle and bustle of the city and the lives that they had left behind. They seemed focused on a higher purpose.

She shook her head to clear it of her strange thoughts. What was happening to her? She knew she should be psyching herself up for the hike ahead and concentrating on searching for something that would make her life more complete, instead of dwelling on the surrealistic quality of the moment.

She took a long drink of the sweet tea and looked up as Haddi began speaking again.

"We will begin by hiking this afternoon to a beautiful garden and then we will camp tonight on a cliff aptly named the Abode of Dust. Our journey will take us through seven valleys," he remarked. "In each valley you will learn valuable lessons about yourself before you pass onto the next valley. On the last day we will scale the Summits of Wonderment and their uppermost peak, Mount Eternity, where those who make the final climb will be rewarded by a treasure of inestimable value found in the temple at the top."

"What kind of treasure?" Richard Malone asked. "Do we get to bring some of it back with us?"

"Of course," Haddi said, with a twinkle in his eye. "But it's not as easy to find as it seems."

"Even if we don't find anything of value," Mary put in, "it will be worth the trip."

Melissa suddenly paid closer attention to what the guide was saying. A treasure? A temple? What a story she would have to tell when she arrived home! Perhaps finding the treasure would make her happy and complete? It would certainly go a long way toward helping her feel she had achieved a goal on this trip. And wouldn't it be nice to watch Dobson eat his words when she brought back something to prove she had made it after all?

After a few minutes, Haddi doused the fire and took the lead as they began their hike out of the sunny meadow and into the fog.

CHAPTER 4

To Melissa, it seemed as though the meadow immediately disappeared. She lost all track of time in the thickening fog. The group hiked, single file, for what could have been minutes or hours. The curtain of white swirled around her, obliterating her surroundings. When Melissa turned around to see how far they had come from the meadow, the meadow was gone, swallowed up in the twisting tendrils of the dense fog. She shivered, even though it wasn't cold.

As Melissa stood there for a moment, contemplating all that she had left behind, she felt someone touch her shoulder.

"Melissa?" Katherine asked. "Are you coming?"

Melissa blinked and focused on Katherine and the present. She looked ahead to where the rest of the group was quickly disappearing up the path.

"I was daydreaming, I guess," Melissa admitted. "This fog is so strange, so forbidding, almost. It's as if the fog is all there is . . . no past, no future, only the here and now. And, it's so quiet. The only thing I can hear is the sound of my own breathing. I can't even judge how far we've walked."

Katherine laughed softly. "Listen!" she whispered.

"We've actually walked quite a distance. We're coming close to the Tree of Being. We should be able to hear the song of the Nightingale of Knowledge. She lives in the highest boughs of the ancient tree."

Melissa strained her ears, but heard nothing.

"Let's walk on a bit further. I think the rest of the group has reached the tree," Katherine remarked.

Melissa's footsteps were muffled on the leaf-strewn path as she followed Katherine deeper into the fog. Up ahead she could faintly make out the blurry outline of a huge, gnarled tree growing majestically beside the path.

As they approached its trunk, Melissa was struck by its grandeur. She had never seen a tree so huge, a tree that appeared to have been rooted in that very spot since the beginning of time. Strong and straight, its ancient trunk was larger around than all of them could reach if they circled it together. Its bark was thick and crusty, yet seemed to pulse with life. She could see why it was called the Tree of Being.

"It's beautiful," Elise exclaimed. "Who could have guessed that such a treasure was so close to the meadow. The fog hides it so well."

"It's probably good that the fog is here to protect this tree," Richard commented. "Can you imagine the number of lumber companies that would like to get their hands on this choice hunk of wood?"

"Oh," Mary said with a wistful sigh. "Cutting it down would be such a tragedy."

"No one will ever cut it down," Haddi declared, "for only those who seek out the Tree of Being with pure hearts will ever find it. Those intent on harming it will never find their way in the mist."

"I find that hard to believe," Melissa whispered to

Katherine. "The path led us right to it."

Katherine smiled and pointed back along the path they had followed. "What path?" she asked.

Melissa stared hard at the soft, springy ground. Where a moment before she had followed a well-worn track, now she saw only layers of leaves and moss. The path was gone!

She looked up into the spreading canopy of the tree, wondering about its ancient mysteries. How many others had stood in awe where she was standing and pondered history in its lofty branches? What secrets would the tree reveal if it could talk to the wayfarers beneath it?

Suddenly, in the silence of her contemplation, she heard a sweet, lilting warble. Letting her eyes follow the silvery sound, Melissa spotted a nightingale, perched on one of the uppermost branches, her beak lifted in song.

"Oh!" Mary breathed. "The Nightingale of Knowledge!"

"I wondered if we would see her," Elise added breathlessly. "I really hoped we would."

"Listen," Katherine said. "The Dove of Certitude is answering from the Bower of the Heart."

Sure enough, immediately after the nightingale warbled out her tinkling tune, a cooing reply floated to their ears from a bower of wild roses surrounding the clearing that the Tree of Being dominated.

"It sounds as if they are talking to each other," Mary whispered. "I wonder what they are saying."

"They sound like bird songs to me," Melissa said, wondering what everyone was getting so excited about. And another thing: why did all of the trees and bowers and birds have special names?

She was about to ask Katherine or Haddi when

suddenly Haddi began reciting: "*And I praise and glorify the first sea which hath branched from the ocean of the Divine Essence, and the first morn which hath glowed from the Horizon of Oneness, and the first sun which hath risen in the Heaven of Eternity, and the first fire which was lit from the Lamp of Pre-existence in the lantern of singleness: He who was Aḥmad in the kingdom of the exalted ones, and Muḥamad amongst the concourse of the near ones, and Maḥmúd in the realm of the sincere ones. '. . . by whichsoever (name) ye will, invoke Him: He hath most excellent names' in the hearts of those who know. And upon His household and companions be abundant and abiding and eternal peace!*"

"What in heaven's name is he talking about?" Melissa asked Katherine.

"Haddi is talking about the Manifestations of God. He's talking about the eternal life of the prophets who have come from God to guide people to the true path. The trip to Mount Eternity is not only a hike up a hill, Melissa; it is a journey into the soul, and a way to strengthen your relationship with God."

"But I don't really have a relationship with God," Melissa admitted. "I've never been very interested in that sort of stuff."

"But God is interested in you," Katherine assured her. "That's why you wanted to come on this trip."

"Sounds a little weird to me," Melissa countered. "If you all expect me to wax eloquent over a tree or hear secret messages in bird songs, it won't work. I'm just not the spiritual type."

Katherine smiled. "Every one of us has a spiritual side, but no two of us are alike in the way we receive spiritual guidance. Maybe the songs of the nightingale and the dove aren't the key for you. Have you smelled the flowers? Some of the most fragrant flowers in the world grow and thrive in this clearing."

Melissa looked doubtful. How could flowers grow in such a damp and misty place? She followed Katherine's example and got down on her knees. There before her was a carpet of delicate white blooms, like morning glories, she thought. A little to her left, nestled in the brilliant green moss, were bunches of miniature blue forget-me-nots, and to her right, tiny red clovers.

She bent down to inhale what she thought would be a weak fragrance from such tiny flowers but, to her surprise, their scent was heavenly. Pure and simple, the little blossoms gave off a perfume worthy of an entire rose garden. And each flower seemed to smell different and unique, even though they grew right beside each other.

"I guess I haven't taken time lately to enjoy the little things," Melissa commented to Katherine. "If Dobson and I had come here together, we probably would have just walked over these flowers without noticing their beauty or their fragrance."

"All of us get too busy in our lives," Katherine said. "It's so easy to forget the small pleasures. Yet, if we open our hearts to God's love, He will show us beauty in even the tiniest plant or insect, or the most minute speck of dust."

"I'm beginning to see that," Melissa said slowly. "When I look at the perfection of these tiny flowers, it makes me feel kind of unimportant in the whole scheme of things."

"Not unimportant," Katherine corrected. "Just as important and significant as any of God's creations. Everything works together to make the whole."

Melissa, still kneeling, reached out to touch the

petals of a perfect miniature red rose. "Look at this beautiful – ouch! It pricked me!"

A single drop of blood, as red as the rose, welled up on her index finger. She watched in fascination as it formed and then fell to the grass below. But it didn't fall on the grass. It spattered onto a marble, heart-shaped plaque almost hidden by the overgrown greenery.

"Katherine, look what I've found," Melissa cried excitedly as she brushed the grass away from the words engraved on the face of the tablet. "It says, *'Fear God, and God will give you knowledge.'*" She looked up, puzzled. "What does that mean? Who carved this and left it here?"

"I don't know," Katherine said, bending down to examine the clean, white tablet nestled in the grass. "But what it says is true. If we follow the clear path to the garden where we camp tonight, and open ourselves to the beauty around us along the way, we'll learn some valuable lessons. Last time I came to this clearing, I found a tablet, too."

"You did? What did your tablet say?" Melissa was confused, but something in her desperately wanted to know more.

"The tablet I found said, *'Walk the beaten paths of Thy Lord!'*"

Melissa looked around and noticed that the rest of their party had gone on ahead while she and Katherine had been smelling the flowers. She remembered that Haddi had said, *'Peace be upon him who followeth the Right Path.'* Paths seemed to be awfully important on the journey to Mount Eternity.

"Do you know the right path now?" Melissa asked, frowning at the empty clearing. "Because it looks as if we've been left behind." She was thinking about the way that the path they had followed to get to the Tree of Being had disappeared.

"The path from here to the cliff where we camp is well trodden," Katherine said. She pointed to a trail leading off from the clearing. The sides of the trail were clearly marked with rock borders and the path itself was dirt, solidly packed.

"What are we waiting for?" Melissa said, starting off along the path. "Let's go ask the others if they found tablets, too."

CHAPTER 5

It wasn't long before the easy-to-follow path that had begun at the clearing began climbing upward. The soft, packed dirt gave way to jagged rocks and boulders, and, although the path was still outlined clearly, Melissa and Katherine found that the going became rougher with each steep step.

"Everything is so desolate," Melissa remarked, taking a moment to catch her breath and look around. "So gray. That's how I feel that my existence has been lately: dull and gray – lifeless."

"Why do you say that?" Katherine asked. "I've seen you around school. You're always surrounded by your friends and your boyfriend. You always seem busy and happy."

"I suppose it looks that way to other people. And, it's true, I'm busy all the time. Dobson and I go out by ourselves or with friends, and track practice takes up a lot of time. And then there are the events I have to attend to promote my father's import business. But all of that seems so superficial. I don't feel as if I'm accomplishing anything, or growing as a person."

Katherine was quiet for a moment. "What I've found by coming on this trip in the past is that nothing seems as bleak and lifeless as it first appears. There is beauty in even the most desolate landscape. There are lessons to be learned and ways to grow even given the most superficial and meaningless of tasks."

"What do you mean by that?"

"The beauty and the lessons come from within. If you depend on outside forces or people to entertain you and give your life meaning, then you will always be disappointed."

"I have to make my own way, in other words," Melissa said thoughtfully. "I suppose I already knew that, and that's why I wanted to come on this trip."

Katherine nodded in understanding. "I think we instinctively know a lot of things, but we ignore them if they seem like too much work."

Melissa laughed and headed off up the path. "That's probably very true." She took a couple of steps and then suddenly bent down to examine a tiny flower growing out of a crack in the rough stone beneath her feet.

A thin shaft of sunlight broke through the fog and touched the delicate purple petals, making them shine. "Look at this flower," Melissa said, reaching out to touch the scalloped leaves. "How easy could it have been for a flower to take root and bloom in the crack of this rock? But, if I was to attribute emotions to plant life, I would say it looks very happy growing here, even though there isn't another flower or blade of grass in sight."

Katherine bent down and admired the stalwart bloom. "There's more than just the unexpected beauty of the flower here," she said. "Look at the rock where it's growing."

Leaning over to look where the roots of the flower had expanded the crack in the rock, Melissa saw a rainbow pattern of colors revealed. "Amazing," she said. "The surfaces of the rocks are all gray, but inside they're filled with colors." She glanced up at the rocks along the side of the path, the boulders strewn around on the barren landscape. At first all she saw was gray, but as her eyes adjusted to the filtered sunlight breaking through the thinning fog, she began to see other cracks, other hidden rainbows.

"Just think, if it hadn't been for that one little flower, I would never have noticed how pretty these rocks really are. And is it my imagination or is the fog lifting?"

"The veils are being drawn away," Katherine said mysteriously. "C'mon. The garden isn't far now. Just over this next rise, I think."

Melissa marveled at how the fog seemed to dissipate as they climbed higher. It was just the opposite of what she had thought would happen. And instead of the temperature dropping, the sun's rays, piercing through the last vestiges of white, warmed her and soon she was taking off her sweatshirt and stuffing it into her backpack.

Though they were still climbing, her feet felt bouncier, her load lighter than it had at the beginning of their trek earlier that afternoon. She decided that her muscles had finally warmed up to the hike after months of sitting behind a desk at school. Track was okay for building short bursts of stamina, but there was nothing like hiking to build endurance. It was too bad that Dobson hadn't come. He might have shaken off some of his overbearing stuffiness.

As soon as she thought about Dobson, she realized that she was glad he hadn't come. Melissa never really felt quite free enough to be herself when she was around him.

"If I had realized how much I needed to get away," she mentioned to Katherine as they cleared the top of the hill and emerged onto a plateau, "I would have made more of an effort to have done so before this . . ."

Her words were cut off mid-sentence as they came to the lip of a shallow protected basin and looked down into a beautiful garden.

"Oh!" Melissa breathed, captivated immediately by the joyful explosion of plant life. "I never dreamed that anything so gorgeous could exist up on top of this hill."

"The Garden of Knowledge is protected from the harsh winds, smiled upon by the life-giving sun, and freshened by the mists," Haddi told them as they descended into the almost tropical paradise.

"But who takes care of it?" Mary asked. "There isn't a weed or a thistle anywhere. It has a wild beauty, yet it's not overgrown."

"There are many of us who tend the Garden of Knowledge, including all of the wayfarers on the journey you are now on. By tasting the fruits of knowledge and casting the seeds to the wind, the garden continues to flourish and grow. So please," Haddi waved his hand to encompass the heavily-laden fruit trees and berry-covered vines, "partake."

Melissa smiled at Katherine. "Suddenly I'm very hungry," she said.

"Me, too."

The girls rushed to the first tree and each picked a huge, juicy peach. Melissa took a bite and let the warm juice run down her chin. It was the most heavenly taste she had ever experienced, perfectly ripe with just the right texture and sweetness. Of course, she knew that hiking a long distance tends to make anything taste good, even powdered eggs and camp-style biscuits, but this peach was different. It seemed almost too good to be true. She looked up to see Katherine enjoying her own peach.

"Delicious, isn't it," Katherine smiled.

"Mmm. None of the exotic fruit my father imports has ever tasted so good. Just think what the supermarkets back home would give for produce like this."

"It would never survive the journey," Katherine said. "The secret to its ripeness is the way it sweetens on the tree until the second you bite into it."

Melissa looked around the garden. As she savored the succulent peach, her eyes took in the profusion of colors and shapes around her. If possible, the garden seemed even more beautiful with each bite she took. Still hungry after finishing her peach and casting the stone away as Haddi had instructed, she reached for a plum, and then a bunch of grapes. She didn't stop to wonder why all of the fruits grew and ripened at the same time in the garden, while in the world outside they ripened at different times throughout the year. She just ate and experienced both the taste of the fruit and the beauty of the garden.

"If I camped here for the rest of the week, I think I would be satisfied for life. Everything is so hectic at home and so peaceful here. I would love just to stay for a few days, eat the fruit, and think about my future," Melissa told Katherine.

"I know what you mean," Katherine said. "It *is* peaceful here."

"This garden makes me realize that there's more to life than pushing buttons and meeting deadlines," Elise said.

"What do you do back in the real world?" Melissa asked.

"I'm a computer programmer on a schedule that won't quit. This is the first vacation I've taken in two years," Elise explained. "All of those rush jobs and important assignments seem so distant now, as if they really didn't matter at all. I've always known that peace of mind is more important than money, but I've been caught up in the rat race for too long. I kept telling myself that someday I would take a moment to enjoy the simple things in life, but someday never came until now."

"It's hard to be detached from the expectations people have for you," Richard said. "At home I'm a son, a husband, an employee and more. People are so attached to titles and how they think a person with that title should behave."

"It really would be nice to live somewhere where people accepted you as you are," Mary added. "If I found a place like that, I would leave everything behind and move there immediately."

"My friends at school think I'm crazy," Melissa told them, "but I've been feeling the same way for quite a while. I don't like the way the rest of the world tries to put me in a predesigned mold. It's almost as if I don't have any choice – my life is already programed for me."

"That's not true, though," Katherine assured Melissa. "You've already taken a big step toward breaking out of the mold by coming on this trip. You've already done and seen things that most people will never get far enough away from their everyday lives to do or see. I've found that my real self is my spiritual self. The most important thing is to live my life in praise of God."

"That's true," Elise commented. "Religion isn't just

something you do every once in a while. Your faith should be a way of life."

"Sometimes I just feel so tired of it all," Melissa remarked, looking around. "I feel like I could just lay down in this plush grass and sleep for a week."

Katherine smiled. "You won't feel that way for long," she said. "The Fruit of Knowledge does strange things to people. It makes them see more clearly and understand things that before seemed impossible to comprehend. But a little knowledge isn't enough. Once you've tasted it, you crave more, you want to move forward and discover what lies ahead."

"After I take a nap," Melissa said and yawned for emphasis. She lay down on the soft, green carpet and closed her eyes. For a few brief moments she felt more relaxed than she had felt in several years. It was as though the beauty of the garden washed over her and began healing the wounds that time and pressure had placed upon her.

Truths became evident. She didn't like the way her life was going. She needed more. She wasn't sure that Dobson and his plans for her were what she wanted. The garden and her new insight into herself seemed to give her permission to let go of the past and reach for a new and very uncertain future with confidence.

When she was finally and truly relaxed and beginning to drift off to sleep, her feet began to tingle. The feeling began in her toes and slowly crept up her legs, into her body and onto her arms and head. Suddenly she wasn't sleepy any more. In fact, she felt perfectly refreshed, as though she had slept for hours, not moments.

She stood up and took a few tentative steps. She felt

as though she was walking on air, so buoyant were her hiking boots. She felt the sudden urge to leap into the air and was certain that if she tried it she would end up flying. Her tiredness had completely gone and she was charged with energy.

Melissa looked around the garden where she had been so content a moment before and, suddenly restless, had the distinct urge to move on. It wasn't that she no longer saw the beauty or felt the peacefulness. She did. But, somehow, she knew there was more. Ahead the tip of Mount Eternity crested above the clouds, serene and beckoning. The seven valleys awaited her and her imagination conjured up even more beautiful landscapes and gardens ahead. Not only that, she would never find the treasure of inestimable value if she stayed in the Garden of Knowledge.

Melissa shouldered her backpack and bounced over to where Katherine was standing. Mary and Richard were just rising from naps of their own and Elise was talking quietly with Haddi.

"Is everyone ready to move on?" Melissa asked when she reached them.

Haddi smiled. "A little knowledge makes one yearn for more. There is much to be learned on the paths and in the valleys ahead. Are you ready?"

Melissa smiled back, no longer afraid of what lay ahead. "I'm ready to learn and experience as much as I can. Mount Eternity, here I come!"

CHAPTER 6

Everyone was in good spirits as they left the Garden of Knowledge. Just her first few experiences so far were enough to convince Melissa that this was a trip like no other. Who would have thought that just beyond the fog, hidden from the eyes of the world, were giant sentinels like the Tree of Being and lush gardens ripe with the Fruit of Knowledge? All her life she had lived so close to these unusual places and things and yet had never known of their existence. Still, the beaten paths were there if anyone chose to follow, if anyone decided to leave the world behind and step into the unknown.

She didn't think that anyone would find their way without a guide and Haddi had been wonderful. He was sympathetic when someone wanted to slow down, encouraging when someone began losing their confidence, comprehensive when another asked an involved question about their surroundings. Above all, he was serene and an inspiration. Melissa made her way to the front of the group to speak to him.

"Is it just me, or does this trek make everyone feel as though they've entered another dimension?" she asked.

Haddi laughed. "Dimensions are just space and time and we all have plenty of each." He lightly stroked the petals of a flower on the side of the path. "People see things differently. Your reality is yours alone. In some ways, the world you exist in is similar to the world others exist in, but in other ways it's completely unique."

"I don't understand," Mary said from behind. She echoed Melissa's thoughts exactly.

"Look at this rose," Haddi said. "What color is it?"

"Red," Mary said.

"Is it red, Melissa?" he asked, turning to her.

"Well," Melissa said, looking carefully. "It seems more on the pink side to me, with a dark maroon color on the edges of the petals."

"Katherine?" Haddi asked.

Katherine smiled. "To me it appears more like a plum tone with a little peach thrown in for good measure."

"As you can see, each person's perception is unique. We're all looking at the same flower, and yet it appears different to each of us." He began walking along the path again.

"So what you're saying is that other people might walk this same path and not even see the Tree of Being or the Garden of Knowledge?" Melissa asked. "That seems impossible! How could anyone miss them?"

"Oh, they would see them," Haddi replied. "But they would not know or appreciate them for what they are. Their beauty and significance would escape them. To some, the Tree of Being would simply be a big tree, and the Garden of Knowledge, a bunch of accidental fruit trees. On this journey you must search deeper, seek meanings beyond the obvious. That is the only way you will find your own center of realities."

At that moment the group emerged from the cover of trees and stood on a barren cliff. The wind buffeted them from the north and thick swirls of dust billowed around their feet. Melissa shivered as the sun went down.

"We will camp here for the night," instructed Haddi.

"But the dust and wind," Mary remarked. "Shouldn't we hike down into the valley or back into the woods for protection?"

"We will find shelter near the stream yonder," Haddi said, pointing a few yards away to a protected alcove of pines surrounding a clear, bubbling stream. "We don't want to tackle the Valley of Search until morning."

Katherine and Melissa walked to the edge of the cliff and peered over into the valley. They took care to brace themselves against the roaring wind.

"The first valley," Melissa said. "I'm so jazzed up. I feel like we're really on the way now. A part of me wishes I was the wind, so that I could rush ahead and not wait for morning."

"I know what you mean. The wind makes me excited, too."

As they stood gazing out over the valley, the girls could make out several parties of searchers, their flashlights scanning the darkness as they wandered about.

"What are they looking for?" Melissa asked.

"They are looking for the traceless friend, the messenger who will give them the fragrance clue that will lead them to the entrance to the second valley."

Overhead the moon rose and illumined the scene from the valley's head where they stood, to the pass at the other end that led onto the next valley.

"Why don't they just head for that pass down there?" Melissa asked, pointing toward the exit.

"It's not that easy," Katherine told her. "From here, high atop the Abode of Dust, the way seems obvious, but down in the Valley of Search it is the quality of the seeking that counts."

"That doesn't make sense," Melissa said. She looked at the moonlit trail that meandered down into the valley and led directly toward the opposite end and the pass. "Just stick to the trail and you're home free."

Katherine shook her head. "Only someone who truly wants to pass into the next valley will succeed, even if all of their companions go on before them."

"You mean that those people down there are doomed to wander around in the valley forever? That sounds a little ominous to me."

"No, no, they'll eventually find their way back to this cliff and either go home or start over and try to make it through the valley again."

"Oh, that's just great! I don't want to come all this way and then have to crawl home in defeat," Melissa said. She knew she must sound a bit sarcastic, but, after all, she had vowed to Dobson that she wouldn't fail. The thought of him so blithely telling her that he'd set a place for her at the table that evening really irritated her. He assumed far too much! And she was determined not to let him win this battle.

"Don't worry," Katherine said with a smile. "We'll make it. We have Haddi's help. If we listen to him and do what he says, the hike will be easy."

Melissa fervently hoped so as she ate the delicious stew and noodles that Haddi prepared from the dried vegetables in their packs. They pulled their sleeping bags around the fire after the meal and settled in for the night. The other travelers seemed inclined to talk, but Melissa's eyelids began to droop immediately.

Everyone has a different way of looking at the world,

she thought.

"I've heard of the Valley of Search," she could hear Elise comment. "People say that if you know what to look for, you'll find it immediately."

"Do you know what to look for?" Richard asked.

"I'm not sure," Elise admitted.

"I think the Valley of Search is symbolic of the search for self," Richard said. "If people know themselves well, then they won't be inclined to detour off the path."

To Melissa, Richard sounded a lot like Dobson at that moment — very sure of his destiny. In a way she envied his certainty.

"Deep down inside I think I know what my real self is like," Elise pondered, "but it has been buried for so many years under my service to others that I'm not absolutely positive."

That sounds like me, Melissa thought. Everyone else's servant.

"Is anyone ever positive about their true nature?" Mary asked. "I feel that I'm always changing, growing, learning new things. I hope I'll always be that way."

"There's nothing wrong with being open to new experiences," Haddi said. "In fact, the ability to change is an admirable quality."

As Melissa drifted off, she listened to Haddi's words and pondered their meaning.

"*The stages that mark the wayfarer's journey from the abode of dust to the heavenly homeland are said to be seven. Some have called these Seven Valleys, and others, Seven Cities. And they say that until the wayfarer taketh leave of self, and traverseth these stages, he shall never reach to the ocean of nearness and union, nor drink of the peerless wine.*"

Was he talking about the obstacles that they would

have to overcome? Did he say something about never reaching the ocean of nearness and union? That couldn't be. Katherine had told her that anyone who truly wanted to hike to Mount Eternity would be given the strength to achieve their goal.

"It is incumbent on these servants that they cleanse the heart – which is the wellspring of divine treasures – from every marking, and that they turn away from imitation," Haddi intoned.

There he was, talking about treasures again, Melissa thought. She knew she should wake herself up to listen more carefully, but her full belly and the warmth of the fire were making her so sleepy. Finally she quit fighting the inevitable, and fell into a dreamless sleep.

Melissa woke early and refreshed the next morning and prepared for her journey by eating a nourishing breakfast of hot cereal topped with fruit carried from the Garden of Knowledge.

Anxious to be on her way, Melissa was ready before anyone else. In the light of day, the exit from the Valley of Search was clearly visible at the far end of the valley. From their lofty vantage point, the path was clear, the goal in sight.

Melissa took a deep breath of the crisp morning air. "I'm ready," she told Katherine. "I feel as if we're really getting down to business now." She pointed down the trail to the valley floor. "The trail isn't too steep and it looks easy," she said. "We should be there by noon, not nightfall. Maybe we'll even make it through two valleys today."

"Anything is possible," Haddi said with a smile. "Of course, the trail is a bit harder than it looks."

Melissa's gaze took in the wide, slightly sloping trail and she didn't say a word. She knew it was going to be a breeze and she was ready to begin.

It seemed like hours later that everyone else was finally packed and ready to go. Haddi went on ahead. Mary and Richard followed him with Elise, and Katherine and Melissa brought up the rear.

"What shall we have for dinner tonight? It's our night to cook, you know," Melissa mentioned to Katherine as they began their hike. "I noticed some biscuit mix in my pack. Maybe we could make pot pies."

Katherine laughed. "You're sure thinking ahead," she said. "We only just ate breakfast."

"I figured that if we planned now, we'd be able to walk further and get well into the second valley before we made camp."

"It's kind of funny," Katherine mused. "I felt the same sort of impatience when I first walked this path, but I learned a valuable lesson along the way that has helped me in everything I do on a daily basis."

"Really?" Melissa asked, finding it hard to believe that a path down a mountainside could teach many profound lessons. It was just a means to an end, as were all of the other seven valleys – the end being Mount Eternity.

"Yes, truly," Katherine replied. "I learned to make the most of each moment of my life, to enjoy each rock, each blade of grass, each stepping stone."

"I've heard all that before," Melissa countered impatiently. "Then you can look forward with anticipation and back without regrets. I have no problem with that. I'm anticipating Mount Eternity, and I know I won't regret hiking as quickly as possible through these valleys to get there."

"Just remember what I said before," Katherine reminded her. "In the Valley of Search, it's the quality of the search, not the quantity or the speed, that will get you through the valley."

"I'll remember," Melissa said, as she marched slowly along behind the others. But she was already thinking again about dinner that night, and the miles she was sure to cover that day – if Haddi would just speed it up a little.

CHAPTER 7

Even at the slow pace that Haddi had set, the path became increasingly difficult. Boulders blocked their way at every turn and they had to make wide detours through the underbrush to avoid them. Within minutes the trees, which were almost nonexistent on the barren cliff, closed in on the travelers and blocked their view of the valley below. The dense foliage also blocked any clear view of the path ahead. Soon Melissa forgot all about what she and Katherine would cook that night as she endeavored to concentrate on simply putting one foot in front of the other while trying not to let Haddi and the others out of her sight up ahead.

What had appeared easy and effortless from above became incredibly arduous as the day wore on. Each time they rounded a bend, Melissa thought surely they must have reached the bottom, only to be met with another stretch of switchback trail leading into another copse of path-hiding trees. Her toes hurt from being jammed into the front of her hiking boots and she was beginning to despair of ever reaching the bottom. More importantly, she was beginning to wonder if they would ever stop for a drink of water.

By the time they had hiked for several hours,

Melissa's thirst was overpowering, but in her haste to leave that morning, she had forgotten to fill her waterbottle. She hated to ask Katherine. Katherine's prediction about how long it would take to descend into the Valley of Search had been all too correct. She didn't need a lecture on not being prepared on top of it.

Of course, in the back of her mind she knew that Katherine would never lecture her on anything; that just wasn't Katherine's style. But at this point she also knew she deserved a lecture on the pitfalls of impetuosity, so she suffered in silence and wished that the next turn in the path would be the last.

Fortunately, even though the next turn wasn't the end, Haddi raised his hand and called a halt to their hike. "We'll pause here and refresh ourselves by the Wellspring of the Heart," he announced. "Please relieve yourselves of your backpacks and gear and we'll eat lunch."

"Lunch?" Melissa cried, looking at her watch for the first time. "I can't believe that it's already lunchtime. We're not even down the mountain yet."

"We're about halfway down," Katherine told her. She motioned for Melissa to join her on a ledge overlooking the valley. "Come, you can see from here."

"Only halfway?" Melissa croaked in disbelief. Her throat was parched, her lips dry, her muscles exhausted. For the first time on the journey she was tempted to call it quits. Down below her the Valley of Search stretched endlessly in the distance. She could no longer see the pass at the other end. All she saw were dense thickets, overgrown copses, a vast and rugged wilderness.

Also, by leaning back and looking up, she could clearly see the cliff where they had camped the night before. The Abode of Dust, by some trick of the light, still appeared to be right above them, as if they had made almost no progress at all. In contrast, the valley floor appeared distant, unreachable. How wrong she had been in her earlier assessment of the situation!

Katherine offered a drink from her water bottle and Melissa accepted it eagerly.

"We'll never make it to Mount Eternity at this rate," Melissa complained when she had eased her thirst. "Can't we speed this up a bit?" she asked Haddi. "We only have a week to hike to the mountain and back."

Haddi smiled. "We'll make it," he said. "Trust in God. Trust in yourself."

"Trust or not," Melissa remarked, "we had better make this a short lunch if we expect to get down to the valley floor by nightfall." She absolutely did not want to be in one of those desolate-looking groups that she and Katherine had seen from the Abode of Dust the night before, wandering around in the Valley of Search by flashlight.

"Relax and enjoy," Haddi said. "Come, sit down by the Wellspring of the Heart and quench your thirst. Our spiritual selves must drink the water of God's hidden mysteries just as our physical selves must quench their thirst with the cool waters of the stream."

More fancy poetry, Melissa thought as she accepted the cup of clear, sparkling water from Haddi's outstretched hand. But before the cup was even halfway to her lips, there was a commotion on the trail below them. What now? Melissa thought. Another delay?

She imagined rock slides and trees falling to block their path. Burros never entered her mind.

"Burros!" she exclaimed. "Where did they come

from?"

"Many wild burros live in the Valley of Search," Katherine remarked. "I saw some the last time I came, too. I've heard people say that the burros helped them through the valley."

"These look like they're more interested in blocking our path," Melissa declared, marching over to the small donkeys that were milling around on the trail. They didn't appear to have any intention of leaving.

"Shoo! Shoo!" Melissa told them. "Either go up or down, but get out of the way! Haddi, can't you do something?"

Haddi walked over to the burros and stroked the neck of the first one. "Sh, sh," he whispered. "It was so nice of you to come. Please, join us for a drink from the Wellspring of the Heart. It's a long climb up the mountain with nothing to drink."

"He acts as if the beasts can understand him," Melissa said to Katherine.

"Maybe he feels that he should appeal to their better natures."

"That's good," Melissa agreed. "Distract them with a drink of water so that they'll move off the path."

"Perhaps," Katherine remarked enigmatically. "Or maybe he has another plan in mind."

Seeing the burros bend their shaggy heads to drink from the bubbling stream reminded Melissa that she still had the cup of water that Haddi had given her in her hand. She lifted it to her lips and quickly drained it.

She was amazed at how refreshing and thirst-quenching the water was. The drink she had taken from Katherine's water bottle had temporarily slaked her thirst, but this spring water was like a total body and mind experience. Not only did she no longer feel thirst, but she no longer felt the burning need to move on. She dipped her cup into the stream again and drank, this time savoring each swallow, letting it run over her teeth and tongue, drop by precious drop. It was so cleansing and fulfilling.

"This is the best water I've ever tasted," she said.

"It's really refreshing, isn't it?" Elise commented. "Compared to this, the water back home tastes awful. This is so pure it's almost magical."

"My thoughts exactly," Mary said. "I had forgotten how wonderful a cup of water could taste, how soothing a drink could be."

A moment later, when Haddi gathered them together to leave, it almost came as a surprise to Melissa. Something about the water had made her realize that she needed to relax and enjoy each moment as it came. She looked up and saw that the burros were back, milling around on the path again. This time they made her smile.

"They're going with us," Haddi explained. "They are willing to carry us and our gear to the valley floor."

He walked over and slipped a loop of cloth loosely around the first burro's neck. "They are very tame and do not need much guidance," he told Richard as he handed him the makeshift reins. "Your burro's name is Forbearance."

Richard mounted his 'steed' and started off down the trail.

Haddi looped cloth around burros for Elise and Mary and handed them the reins also. "Your burro's name is Fortitude," he told Mary. "And yours is Trust," he said to Elise.

Katherine's burro was called Love, and as soon as Haddi handed her the reins she trotted off down the trail after the others.

There were two burros left. Haddi arranged his gear on one and handed the reins of the other to Melissa.

"Does my burro have a name?" Melissa asked.

Haddi smiled. "Your burro has a very special name," he said. "Your steed for this valley is Patience. Without Patience you will reach nowhere and attain no goal."

"I suppose that's a comment on my attitude this morning," Melissa said. "I just worry that we aren't going to have enough time to get to Mount Eternity. I *really* want to make it."

"Don't be downhearted, Melissa," Haddi said softly. "Each person's journey takes exactly as long as is necessary, but you *will* reach Mount Eternity."

"Is that a promise?"

Haddi winked. "It's just a feeling I have about you. Your heart is burdened by events and circumstances in your life, but you have the desire to search for the truth. That is the key to reaching Mount Eternity."

"Sometimes you talk in riddles," Melissa said as she mounted Patience and waited while Haddi mounted his own burro. Side by side they headed off in the direction the others had taken.

"You only met me yesterday, but you seem to know so much about me already," Melissa continued.

"It is easy to see a soul waiting to break free if you know what signs to look for," Haddi said.

"What signs are those?" Melissa asked over the clip-clop of her burro's hooves on the hard-packed trail.

"Some people exist, other people live," Haddi said mysteriously. "People who merely exist are guided by their base natures. It doesn't matter how much money, power or position they have, it is never enough. They rarely think of serving others because they are too busy serving themselves."

Melissa thought about Dobson and his dreams of becoming a lawyer, not to help the downtrodden, but to make enough money to buy a yacht. She thought of her father and all of his acquisitions, even the way he used her coming on this trip as a means to further his status and position in the community.

"But I don't want to be like that," Melissa declared. "I know there has to be more to life than the country club and material success. I just don't know if this God stuff is for me."

"Has there ever been a time when you have felt at peace?"

"In the Garden of Knowledge."

"I don't mean while on this trip," Haddi said. "How about at home?"

Melissa thought about that for a moment. Then she said, "Sometimes, when I'm running out on the track, I feel so free, so at one with myself and the world around me. Then I come off the track and all of my other obligations and responsibilities press in on me. It seems as if everyone wants a piece of me. My parents want me to be the perfect daughter. My boyfriend wants me to be his unquestioning sidekick. My teachers want me to get good grades. No one asks what I want and I'm not sure what I would tell them if they did."

"It is good that you didn't let any bond hold you back, or allow the opinions of others to deter you from coming on this trip."

Melissa shook her head. "I didn't really think about it

that way. I just knew that I wanted to do this for *me*, and it didn't matter whether they approved or not."

As she was speaking, they emerged onto a flat plateau and she saw Katherine and the others waiting in a little circle up ahead. Behind them rose the mountain they had just descended and Melissa marveled at how the second half of their journey had lasted only moments, yet by distance it was no shorter than the first half. She and Haddi had talked the whole time and she hadn't once felt impatient or in a hurry. She started to ask Haddi why, but he held up his hand.

"As we continue on our journey, perhaps you will find the answers that you seek," Haddi said. He waved his hand in a gesture that encompassed the plateau around them with its waving grass and small prairie shrubs. "This is the Plain of Heedlessness. You must find your own way to the Realm of Being. As we enter the Valley of Search remember to seek only the truth. Let nothing distract you. I will start you on your search, but then you must find your own way. Seek everywhere, even in the most unlikely spot, so that you shall be fortunate enough to find the way to the City of Love in the Valley of Love."

"Will we be successful?" Mary asked anxiously. "It would be so disappointing to come this far and then not find our way."

She had again echoed Melissa's thoughts exactly, and probably everyone else's as well. But Melissa didn't say anything. Somehow she knew, after talking with Haddi, that he could not predict their success. The ardor needed to find the way had to come from within each one of them.

"*Whoso seeketh out a thing with zeal shall find it*," Haddi replied. Then he smiled at all of them. "Let us refresh ourselves again with the water from the Wellspring of the Heart and partake of the fruit of knowledge. Then we must be on our way.

CHAPTER 8

"It looks easy enough," Melissa remarked to Katherine a few moments later when they were all shouldering their packs again for their trek through the Valley of Search.

"This valley is very deceptive," Katherine commented. "Nothing is as it seems. Once you enter, it's like a maze."

"I promise I won't be in a hurry this time," Melissa said. "I'll take my time and pay attention to where I'm going."

"That was the first lesson I learned when I came on this journey, too," Katherine said. "To accept life as it comes and not try to take short cuts or skip whole sections so that I can get results faster. There's no short cut to getting in touch with your true self. It takes time and dedication and *lots* of patience."

"Let's go!" Haddi called. "Once again," he added when the entire group was assembled, "remember to avoid imitations. Search for the Traceless Friend who will give you the fragrance clue that will lead you to the City of Love."

"I didn't know there was a city out here," Melissa said, amazed that she had never heard of it before.

"It's beautiful," Katherine said, her eyes sparkling

with remembrance. "And the people there are so nice, so friendly."

"I can't wait to see it," Melissa said, then popped her hand over her mouth. "I mean, however long it takes, I'll be looking forward to seeing it."

Katherine grinned. "I'll see you there."

Melissa didn't immediately understand why Katherine sounded as if she was saying goodbye. All that talk about becoming separated and each person completing their search on their own was just talk, wasn't it? So long as Melissa kept up with the others, she wouldn't get lost or stray from the path. And she intended to keep up.

Almost immediately, though, her perception of the Valley of Search changed. The moment she walked into the woods, the Plain of Heedlessness disappeared behind her and so did the mountain with its looming cliff, the Abode of Dust. The trees, which had appeared small from the cliff, grew tall and totally blocked the view of the other side of the valley. The trunks were packed so tightly together that no clear path was visible beyond the faint shuffling aside of leaves by her companions in front of her.

She strained to hear Haddi's words from the front of the line. "You must sacrifice all things you have seen, heard and understood and enter the realm of spirit. You must cast away the world and get in touch with your inner selves, then reach out for guidance from the Invisible Realm. There are many people wandering in the valley today. You may meet them on your search."

His voice faded away as he walked faster ahead of them. Melissa hurried to catch up. In her haste, she stumbled over a tree root and sprawled flat on the ground. The fall knocked the wind out of her and when she finally rose, the others were nowhere in sight.

"Katherine!" she called, but her voice came back to her, muffled by the trees. "Hey, wait up!"

No one answered or came back for her.

"No problem," Melissa said to herself. "I'll just follow their trail."

She studied the ground in front of her and could just make out the depressions in the leaves caused by the recent passage of booted feet. She looked up and spotted the sun, shining down through the trees leaving dappled shadows at her feet.

"All right. I'm going east. If I keep heading east, I'll find the way, because the pass to the Valley of Love was at the east end of the Valley of Search."

Talking to herself made her feel better. It also made her feel more confident about her abilities as a hiker. If she kept her back to the sun, path or no path, she would eventually come out at the other end of the valley.

But keeping her back to the sun was easier said than done. Soon the trees grew even closer together and a thick canopy of vines stretched between them, blocking out the late afternoon sun. She tried to keep her bearings by spotting a tree in the distance and then walking toward it, then fixing her gaze on a berry bush further on, and after that a rock outcropping, and so on.

For a while it seemed as if she was making progress, until she came upon what looked like the same berry bush she had spotted in the beginning. When she came again to a familiar rock outcropping, she knew that she was hopelessly lost.

"Why did I ever think this valley would be simple?" she asked herself. It didn't seem to matter that she was using all of her skills as a cross-country hiker. Her skills and sense of direction were useless. Everything she had known in the past had brought her around in a circle. Now she was back where she started and there was no sign of any Traceless Friend, or fragrance clues, or even any other searchers. Had all the others stayed together and already found the way to the City of Love? Were they all sitting comfortably in some restaurant, laughing about how long it was taking her?

A part of her mind screamed at the injustice of it all, another part chastised herself for ever thinking she could make it to Mount Eternity at all, a third part told her that maybe she was holding onto old notions of right and wrong and that she needed to let go.

It was the third part that finally won out. She decided that the other people in her group would never laugh at her expense and that, just as Haddi had said, everyone was completing their search on their own. She needed to stop trying to outsmart the valley with her hiking and tracking skills. Instead she needed to search for the Traceless Friend and the fragrance clue.

Almost immediately, the minute she decided to give herself over to the valley, a person walked across the path in front of her.

"Hello!" she called. "Are you the Traceless Friend?"

"No," the man called back. "I'm searching, too."

"Do you know which way is east?" Melissa asked him.

He pointed back over his shoulder. "But, it's a dead end. You won't find the pass there."

"I'll give it a try anyway," Melissa said. "Thank you."

A moment later the man disappeared into the trees. She walked briskly in the direction he had pointed out and soon came to an almost vertical rock wall.

"Could I have walked as far as the east end of the valley already?" she asked herself. "Are these the mountains that the pass cuts between?"

She followed along the wall for a distance, searching for the pass, but the wall was impenetrable. She saw a woman up ahead of her, touching the wall with her hands, and rushed to her side.

"Do you know where the pass to the Valley of Love is?" she asked the woman. "I've been searching and searching, but I've come up against this wall and there doesn't appear to be a way through. I certainly can't climb it."

"I know," replied the woman. "It's frustrating, isn't it? You might try back there by that stream," she suggested. "At least the water is good, and the flowers smell lovely. It's a nice place to rest while you try to puzzle out a solution."

"Thanks," Melissa said. While she wasn't tired, she *was* very interested in the thought of the flowers. Flowers had a fragrance. Perhaps they were a clue. At this point she was willing to try anything. Though it wasn't night yet, she knew it was getting late and visions of wandering around in the valley with her flashlight filled her mind again.

The stream wasn't that far from the rock wall. When she reached it she bent down to drink. The water was as cool and refreshing as the woman had said and the flowers were as beautiful. Wood peonies, narcissi, crocuses and impatiens bloomed along the banks of the sparkling stream. Their fragrances filled the air in the clearing and Melissa bent to smell each one in turn.

The impatiens had a particularly delicate scent and Melissa lingered over them. A small trail of impatiens led off into the woods and Melissa followed them, thinking that maybe she had found the fragrance clue. To her dismay, the flowers dwindled and then finally disappeared altogether back at the base of the same rock wall she had just come from. Since she knew the wall was solid, she lifted her nose and followed another wispy trail of scent, this time pine.

Unfortunately, her nose only led her to another section of the wall. She was beginning to despair. Then she spotted an old woman up ahead sitting on the stump of a fallen tree.

"Excuse me," she said, "are you the Traceless Friend?"

"No, indeed," the woman said, smiling and pointing her wrinkled hand toward a clump of hawthorn bushes. "You must follow that curve of path over there. That will take you to the right spot."

"Thank you," Melissa said with a sigh. Finally she was getting somewhere. She hurried to the stand of hawthorn and followed the faint, curving path. Scents assailed her from all directions and she wasn't sure which to follow first. She left the trail to discover the source of a sweet, pungent odor, and a few steps later, found that the smell dissipated into thin air. She branched off the trail again to follow a whiff of honeysuckle, but that, too, vanished the moment she left the path.

Again and again a particular fragrance drew her from the path and she searched for each one, only to find that the scent disappeared, or that her way was blocked by a section of the rock wall.

While she was searching, night fell, and with it her doubts and fears returned full force.

I'll never get out of here, she thought, turning on her flashlight. I'm going to be lost in this valley forever.

Twenty years from now they'll find my skeleton. It will probably still be wandering around, looking for the Traceless Friend. Hey, maybe the Traceless Friend is a skeleton – or a ghost. That would be traceless, all right.

Her thoughts flew in as many directions as her feet. First determined to beat the valley, then resigned to being lost forever, Melissa wandered for hours. She lost all track of time, of direction, of distance. Once she stopped to eat a snack from her pack, but she wasn't really hungry. What did food matter, with her whole future at stake?

Finally, she came to a small clearing and sank down on the soft carpet of moss. She had tried everything she knew, used every skill, followed every lead, and had still found nothing. As a last resort she began to pray.

"Lord, I need help," she began. "I haven't talked to you in a long time. I'm not sure I even believe that you can hear me. But I'm totally lost and I have nowhere else to turn."

Melissa closed her eyes and thought about everything that had happened that day. She had started out at the top of the Abode of Dust, certain that the downhill path and the trek through the Valley of Search would be a cinch. The way to the pass had looked so foolproof from the heights: just head east and aim for the mountains.

The downhill path had turned out to be much more time-consuming and treacherous than she had imagined. She had learned that without patience she would reach nowhere and attain no goal. It seemed like forever since she had said goodbye to her trusty burro, Patience, on the Plain of Heedlessness.

On the plain she had listened to Haddi talk about letting go of preconceived notions, of avoiding imitations, of finding her own way through the valley, but she hadn't paid much attention because she had been planning to stay with the others and follow them all the way through the valley.

Then that stupid root had tripped her, and the others had left her behind. Since then she had been wandering, searching, asking others and meeting one dead end after another until her frustration and exhaustion had brought her to her knees.

"Please, Lord, I need you. Help me find my way out of here. No, forget that. What I mean is, help me do what you want me to do. I am your servant."

Melissa bowed her head then and waited for an answer. She listened to the chatter of a family of raccoons washing their food in the stream. She felt the night breeze rise around her and gently caress her aching muscles. She let the darkness and solitude creep in on her, and still she sat, waiting, hoping, praying for an answer.

Melissa wasn't aware of how long she knelt on the soft moss. She only knew that as time went on her anxieties melted away and she felt suspended in a warm, comforting presence. No words came to her, yet she felt a stirring within, an answer waiting to burst forth.

Eyes closed, she continued to meditate. And then the answer came. She wasn't sure if she was remembering Haddi's words, or if she was putting together the pieces of the puzzle herself from things she had heard before, but suddenly she knew that she was being protected, that God had not abandoned her.

It's the quality of the search that is important, not the reaching of the goal, she thought. Even if it takes years of dead ends and misdirected side trips, God will never test me beyond my endurance. And eventually, when I no longer worry about the goal, I will simply find it.

She basked in the warmth of her newly acquired knowledge for a few moments longer, then opened her eyes. In front of her, as if she had always been there, was a lovely woman, sitting peacefully beside a small fire.

"Come, join me," the woman said. "Would you like some tea?"

CHAPTER 9

"Thank you," Melissa said, accepting the cup of steaming tea. She sipped some of the warm liquid and let its honeyed sweetness swish around in her mouth before she swallowed. "Who are you?"

"A friend, a fellow seeker like yourself," the woman said. "Do not despair. *Whoso seeketh out a thing with zeal shall find it.*"

"I've been searching for the Traceless Friend and the fragrance clue that will lead me into the Valley of Love, but I've only found dead ends and false trails. But that doesn't matter any more," Melissa said, and realized that she meant it. "I know that God will not test me beyond my endurance and I'm sure I could find a bunch more places to search, if that is what would please Him."

"If all who came into this valley had your attitude, their journey would be much shorter," the woman said.

Melissa sipped her tea, letting it refresh her. If anyone had told her yesterday that she would be sitting in the dark with a woman she didn't know, drinking tea and talking about God, she would never have believed them. But by the glow of the small fire, the Valley of Search seemed more of a comforting presence than a hurdle to overcome. Moving onto the next valley didn't seem as important now as discovering everything she could about the valley she was in.

"Thank you for saying so," Melissa said, "even though it has taken me all day and night to realize that. I just hope that my friends aren't worried about me."

"Your friends understand that each person must complete his or her own search. Your realizations in the Valley of Search must be your own."

"That makes sense in a funny sort of way," Melissa said. "I think people must be shown something to have it sink in. Words mean nothing, unless there are actions behind them. For example, my boyfriend didn't want me to come on this trip. He was convinced I would fail and be at his house for dinner last night. I told him I was going, but he wouldn't believe me."

"I should think he believes you now," the woman said. "What about you? What do you believe?"

"I'm beginning to believe in things that I thought I could do without."

"Such as?"

"God, for one thing," Melissa said. "Since coming on this journey, I think I'm starting to believe in God, or at least in some kind of creative force that is grander than we are. I'm not sure why, but I'm not going to analyze it right now."

"Anything else?" her companion asked.

Melissa thought for a second and then nodded her head. "I think I'm beginning to believe in myself."

The woman laughed and her laughter blended with the trickling sound of the water pouring over the rocks in the stream. "You are much further on your search than you realize," she said.

"Really?" Melissa looked around at the clearing and

rubbed her fingers over the soft grass. "I don't know where I came from or where I'm going. I'm not sure how long I've been here and I don't know how long I'll be staying. It's strange that I'm not worried about that."

"Trust in yourself," the woman said. "Trust in God and let go of all preconceived notions, including those of time and place, of then and now. The passageway to the City of Love has always been near you."

Melissa turned around and looked quickly behind her. Near me? she thought. Where could it be? She turned back to the woman to ask what she meant, but just as suddenly and quietly as she had appeared, she had gone.

Melissa thought to call out her name, but realized she had never given it. Even the fire, which only moments before had heated her tea, was gone without a trace. All that was left was the scent of violets.

It must be her perfume, Melissa thought as she rose to follow the aroma. Not that she thought it would lead her anywhere, but the perfume was so tantalizing, so heady, that she wanted to breathe it in for the pure joy of the experience.

As she walked, a well-worn path appeared between the trees. It led her past the stream and back to the rock wall, still as solid and unyielding as it had been the last dozen times that she had circled back to it.

This time, however, as she left the forest behind and approached the stone face of the cliff, she closed her eyes and forced herself to let go of all of her notions of hard and soft, of direction, of time and distance.

It was so hot near the rock, and so bright. It was almost as if . . . she looked up. Yes, the sun had burst through the fog and was bathing her in its early morning light. She had spent all day and all night in the Valley of Search and now it was morning again. The sun's brightness and heat intensified as she approached the wall, and the violet perfume seemed to fill the air around her.

In front of her the slick rock attracted her, drawing her nearer. She had passed it a dozen times in her search, but it had never seemed so beautiful, so shiny and iridescent. She was pulled toward it as though by a magnet and the urge to touch the heated stone was almost overpowering. Suddenly she knew that she had to touch it. She had to explore its crystal quartz veins and ebony streaks of obsidian. What did it matter if this wasn't the way to the City of Love? She might as well explore the wall just for the sake of exploring it.

Melissa reached out to touch the wall, prepared to stroke the smooth stone, but to her surprise it wasn't smooth. It wasn't even solid. Her hand slipped from sight into a crack in the wall that had been completely hidden by the illusion of the sun shining on the slick surface of the stone.

How many times had she passed right by this very spot and not seen the opening? Hoping against hope, she put her hand, then her arm, and then her whole body into the narrow passageway. It wasn't just a cave, Melissa realized as soon as she stepped inside. It was the pass, the pass she had been searching for, and within moments she stepped straight into what she hoped was the Valley of Love.

It was! She knew she had reached her goal, because all of her friends were there: Katherine, Richard, Mary, Elise and Haddi. They had all made it through the valley and were waiting for her. Behind them, through an old-fashioned, carved archway, was a magnificent city. It wasn't a metropolis like New York or Chicago, but more like a sculpture in glass and chrome, each building more beautiful and shiny than the one next to it.

Melissa was still staring in awe when Katherine ran forward to embrace her. "Welcome! You're just in time for breakfast."

"It's a good thing, too," Mary teased. "You have the powdered cocoa mix."

Melissa hugged each of them in turn. "I'm so glad to see you all," she said. "I was afraid you had gone on without me."

Elise drew her to the fire. "We're in this together," she said. "Come, eat with us, and tell us about your search."

"This is the Valley of Love, and that's the City of Love, isn't it?" Melissa asked.

Katherine nodded.

Melissa sank down by the fire and took the cocoa out of her backpack. "I was beginning to wonder if I would ever find my way out," she told the others as she measured out the powder into the cups. "But after a while it didn't seem to matter any more. I could have gone on searching for ever and probably been content. It's funny, but the moment I stopped worrying about finding the pass, I practically fell into it."

Haddi smiled. "For many, finding the City of Love is like finding God, for the Realm of the Spirit is always there, should you want to accept it."

"There you go, talking about the realm of the spirit and all that abstract stuff," Melissa said. "It's true that I'm beginning to feel that there are other forces at work in the universe besides little old me, but I'm not sure I'm ready for all this God talk. I mean, how am I supposed to understand something that I can't see, or touch?"

"God is our creator," Elise said simply. "I've never doubted it. I know that God helped me through the Valley of Search because the path always seemed clear, the way ahead firmly fixed."

"Really?" Melissa asked.

"Yes," Elise replied. "When I asked God for help, He showed me the way."

"God actually pointed out the pass to you?" Melissa asked incredulously.

Elise shook her head. "Not exactly. I just had faith that I would find it."

"How about you, Mary?" Melissa asked.

"I got lost right away," Mary told her. "I only found my way out a moment before you did. I spent the whole time in a maze of caves and caverns."

"Really?" Melissa said. "I didn't even see a single cave."

"I did," Richard said, "but I decided to go around them and ended up in this weird, swampy area. Look at my boots. I came out only a few minutes before Mary."

Melissa looked down at Richard's feet and indeed they were covered with green slime. "I didn't see the swamp either. I spent all of my time trying to get through that huge rock wall. At least I'm glad I'm not the only one who took so long."

"It wouldn't matter if you were," Katherine said. "Sometimes it takes me longer to get through that valley than other times. What's important to me is that I don't get hooked into following a furrow someone else has ploughed, but concentrate instead on making my own way. We each have our own capacity and our own qualities to develop. God can help us find our path in life just as He helped each of us through the Valley of Search."

"This is too much for me," Melissa said. "I've learned a lot on this trip already. I've learned to have patience. I've become close to all of you, my new friends. And I have to admit that I, too, finally resorted to prayer in the Valley of Search, and experienced a real feeling of contentment. But I'm not sure God or my prayers had anything to do with me finding the pass. More likely it was luck. As for God, I want proof."

Haddi stirred the cocoa in his cup and looked thoughtfully at Melissa. "You must seek the answers to your questions," he said. "Without obstacles to overcome, the treasure would be worthless."

There he was, talking about treasure again.

"But as for proof that God exists, God is immeasurably beyond mere mortal attempts at proofs," Haddi went on. "It might help, though, if I tell you a little story."

Melissa sat back, sipped her cocoa and waited.

"Once there was a renowned scientist. His theories were brilliant, his dissertations were extraordinary. For him, science was a concrete, indisputable way of looking at the world. For every action there was a reaction. For every piece of existence, a scientific explanation. He believed in what he could see, hear and touch; therefore he did not believe in God."

"A very logical man," Mary commented. "What happened?"

"One day, a colleague of his invited him to view a model of the universe and when the scientist saw the intricate and exact duplicate of everything known to man displayed in perfect detail and scale, he was suitably impressed," Haddi explained. "He complimented his colleague on the fine piece of work. 'Who made it?' he asked.

"The colleague smiled and said, 'No one.'"

"No one?" Melissa interrupted. "How can that be? It had to get there somehow. A model like that doesn't just appear out of thin air."

"Exactly," Haddi said, smiling. "The colleague told his scientist friend that there can be no creation without a creator. Therefore, existence alone proves that a creator exists. The model had to have a builder. The world had to have a creator."

"God?" Melissa asked.

"By whatever name," Haddi replied enigmatically.

CHAPTER 10

After breakfast the group took a short rest. All of the travelers were exhausted from their all-night treks through the Valley of Search. Only Haddi and Katherine had walked straight toward the pass, but then this wasn't the first journey for either of them. Of course it became easier the more times one did it.

As anxious as she was to explore the City of Love, Melissa fell asleep almost immediately, her back propped up against her backpack. As she was drifting off, she thought briefly of the past twenty-four hours, how full they had been, how different from anything she had imagined.

She was really glad that she had come on this trip, and if they got busy and didn't stay overlong in the City of Love or in the rest of the Valley of Love, they could still make Mount Eternity and get home by the end of the week.

A city, she mused in her half-awake, half-asleep state. A city this close to home that almost no one has ever heard about, concealed by the mist and the forest. She hoped that when she awakened from her slumber, she wouldn't find that it had all been a dream and that she was still stuck in the clearing by the stream, next to the rock wall, in the Valley of Search.

"Melissa, wake up!" Katherine called through the haze of her dreamstate. "Haddi says it's time to go into the city."

Melissa opened her eyes and found herself staring at the ground. She had bent over in her sleep and her neck was twisted almost off her backpack. Her right leg was stuck out at an odd angle to compensate and her arm was braced against a rock to hold her up.

"Wow," she said. "I must have been really tired."

"We all were," Katherine said. "I slept like a log myself, but I'm ready to see the city now. It looks different from the last time I was here. But, then, it always does. Different lessons to be learned, you know."

Melissa wasn't paying much attention to Katherine's revelations. She was too busy trying to get up. Her neck was stiff and when she tried to bend her leg over to get onto her hands and knees, pain shot across her back.

"Aaaah!" she groaned. "I must have pulled something."

"Need some help up?" Katherine asked.

"No thanks. I'd better do this myself," Melissa said. She gritted her teeth and slowly inched her way over onto her knees. The pain in her back was excruciating. It reminded her of those times when her father bent over incorrectly to pick up a heavy statue and couldn't get up. But she was too young to throw her back out, wasn't she? And she couldn't afford to be out of commission for weeks.

"Are you okay?"

"Not really. I must have slept wrong. My neck and back are killing me. I'm not sure I can get up, much less explore the city."

Katherine held out her hand.

Melissa took it and rose painfully to her feet. That's when she discovered the blisters. "Aaaah!" she cried again.

"What now?" Katherine asked with concern.

"My feet," Melissa told her, wincing against the sting. "I must have gotten blisters from all that walking yesterday."

"I have some ointment and moleskin to treat them with in my pack," Katherine offered.

"Thanks."

Melissa stiffly eased herself down on a nearby rock, not too high, not too low — she wasn't taking any chances. She watched the others prepare to break camp and noticed that everyone was holding their neck or shoulder or leg.

"We're all in great shape," she muttered sarcastically as Katherine returned and handed her the first-aid supplies.

"But the City of Love is so beautiful," Katherine went on, undaunted, "that it will make you forget your pains."

For the first time since she woke up, Melissa turned and looked at the city. The mid-morning sun, glinting off the shiny buildings, was reflected back to her with the brightness of a thousand mirrors. She put her hand up to shield her eyes, which had spent the past day and night adjusting to the dimness of the Valley of Search.

"I can barely see," Melissa said. "Maybe you all had better go on without me until I can loosen up my muscles and get adjusted to daylight again. I'll only slow you down." She turned away from the flashing brilliance of the city and bent over her feet again. Tears formed in her eyes, but she wouldn't let them fall. She didn't want

Katherine to know how much she wanted to explore the city. She was trying to be noble and not hold the others up.

Katherine looked down at her for a moment, then squatted to see her face. "What kind of attitude is this from Westridge High's top track star? If you have a little sprain or a strain in the middle of a track meet, do you quit? Do you pull out of the race and let the other team win?"

"Of course not," Melissa admitted.

"Then what are you doing now?" Katherine asked. "Pretend this is a track meet. No pain, no gain, right? You wanted to reach Mount Eternity and show that boyfriend of yours that you could do it, right? Well, if you don't press on, despite the pain, you'll never make it."

Melissa grinned in spite of her stiff neck. "Yes, coach! I hear you, coach!"

Katherine grinned back. "That's better."

Melissa dragged herself to her feet and hobbled over to put on her backpack. The weight of it on her sore back almost pulled her back down again, but she steeled herself against the pain and managed to turn back to Katherine with a smile.

"Is everyone ready?" Haddi asked.

Murmurs of assent went around the circle. Melissa could tell that everyone else was in pain too.

"Let's go," Melissa forced herself to say brightly.

"I'm with you," Katherine agreed, and started off toward the City of Love.

It wasn't until Katherine had started walking that Melissa noticed she was limping also.

"You, too?"

"A sprain, I think," Katherine said. "I twisted it on a

rock when I was coming through the pass. It doesn't bother me too much until I carry a load."

Melissa chuckled. "What a great impression we'll make in the City of Love."

"What you look like, or feel like, none of your physical imperfections matters in the City of Love," Haddi told them. "Whatever you have seen and heard and understood, you must regard as nothing if you wish to enter the City of Love. Once you taste the honeyed sweetness of reunion with God, you will cast away the world."

"Lucky thing that it's our spirits God is interested in, not our bodies," Katherine remarked cheerfully.

"Lucky thing," Melissa echoed, feeling better despite her aches and pains.

Their camp was only about half a mile from the city's gates and before long they all stood in front of the arched entryway.

"I've never seen anything like it before," Elise commented. "Look at the intricate carving!"

"The detail is exquisite!" added Richard.

"It's incredible," Mary said.

"And such a well-kept secret," Melissa said. "I can't believe this beautiful city is here and that no one in Seaside knows about it. Don't the people living here have to go out to shop or work?"

"Actually the City of Love is completely self-sufficient," Haddi explained. "There are farms, mills, shops, schools, a center for the arts, everything in fact that anyone living here could need."

"No cars, I see," Melissa commented.

Katherine nodded. "There's no need. You can walk everywhere. Come on, let's take a tour."

Actually, a car ride about now would have been nice, Melissa thought. The half-mile walk from their camp had been painful at best. The closer they had got to the city, the worse the glare off the sunlit buildings had become. Her neck hurt more than ever and her back was becoming stiffer by the moment. The blisters on her feet stung with every step.

She continued to suffer in silence because she knew that everyone else was suffering too. And really, what good would it have done to complain? Besides, the city *was* beautiful. She had never imagined the existence of something so perfect, and wondered about the people who lived there all the time.

As if to answer her question, a couple came out to meet them the moment they stepped beneath the carved archway.

"Welcome," the man and the woman said together. He was tall, with dark hair and skin and shiny black eyes. His companion was equally tall, yet fair, with light skin and hair. Her eyes were a piercing cobalt blue. At least Melissa *thought* they were blue.

"Thank you," Melissa said, and heard the others murmuring greetings also.

"My name is Gregory, and this is Cielo. Your group is most welcome in the City of Love. Please, feel free to look around, eat, refresh yourselves and rest."

Melissa wished she could see him better. His voice was so melodious that she knew his expression must be friendly, but her eyes were closed to the thinnest slits against the glare. She was seeing everything through the curtain of her eyelashes, her brow furrowed against the pain in her neck and back.

This is almost like being blind, she thought as she

stumbled along after their guide. I'm in a beautiful city, and yet I can barely see it.

She found she could sense it, though. She could smell the freshness carried on the scent of flowers in the humid air. Everything was so clean. She didn't trip over a single piece of garbage on the sidewalk, or touch a single grimy handrail.

Along their path were shiny brass plaques with written messages and quotes from all of the world's great religions.

Richard read the first one aloud. "'The Lord our God is one Lord.' Jesus Christ, The New Testament, Mark 12:29."

"'But just how many gods are there . . . ? One.' Hinduism, Brihan-Aranyaka Upanishad 3:9:1," read Elise.

Melissa stepped up to the third one. "'He is God, the One and Only: God the Eternal, Absolute . . . and there is none like unto Him.' Muhammad, Koran 112:1-4."

"'No God is there beside Thee, the Supreme ruler, the All-Glorious, the Omniscient.' Bahá'u'lláh, Prayers and Meditations," Mary said.

"'I am the Lord, and there is none else, there is no God beside Me,'" Haddi read. "That quote is from the Old Testament and Judaism."

"And there's one from Buddha," Katherine said. "It says, 'Do not be angry, nor should ye secret resentment bear, for as a mother risks her life and watches over her child, so boundless be your love to all, so tender, kind and mild.'"

"When I hear these quotes," Melissa said, "all of the religions seem in harmony. That's exactly opposite to what I've always been taught. For my parents, there is only one way, and all the others are wrong and misguided. They won't even let me investigate other faiths."

"But as you can see, religion is progressive," Katherine commented. "Each of God's revelations, whether Buddhist, Zoroastrian, Christian, or whatever, are true religions and a part of God's plan for mankind."

"I've never thought of it that way," Elise said, "but progressive revelation makes sense."

"At different times throughout history humankind has needed God's guidance to renew its faith and to give teachings appropriate to specific needs. As we mature, God continues to reveal more to us," Haddi said. "In this age, the unity of humankind is of paramount importance."

"How true," Mary added. "Sometimes I feel as if the world is on the brink of self-destruction."

"I wonder what will have to happen before people sit up and take notice," Richard said. "The City of Love seems a welcome respite from the real world."

"Welcome travelers," a man's voice greeted them from the open doorway of a shop. "Come in, look around," he invited.

Mary and Richard decided to go in, so the rest of the group did, too. Inside the shop, Melissa was able to open her eyes and found that she was standing in an art gallery. All around her, displayed on tables and shelves and hanging from the walls and ceilings were beautiful examples of glass sculpture, paintings, carved wooden statues and woven tapestries.

"My dad would do just about anything to import this kind of art," Melissa whispered to Katherine.

"It's gorgeous, isn't it?" Katherine remarked.

"Is it for sale?"

"No, just for display. Every time I've come here there have been different pieces, different examples of the work of the people who live here."

"Art, simply for the enjoyment of it," Melissa murmured thoughtfully. "Quite a different concept from the commercialism back home. Why don't the artists sell their work?" she asked the man who had invited them in.

"The people who live in the City of Love are happy to share their work with anyone who wants to look at it, but it has no commercial value to them because we don't use money here."

"You mean people don't work?"

"Yes, everyone works to their capacity. Artists create art, farmers farm, tailors sew. In the whole Valley of Love, work has been elevated to the station of worship. We work to serve God and serve humanity, and what we produce is shared equally."

"I like this concept," Melissa said. "I'm so tired of people trying to tell me that my goal in life should be to make money and accumulate things."

"That's how it is in the world," Katherine commented. "And, really, there's nothing wrong with working hard, making money and acquiring things. God put everything on this earth so that people could enjoy it. We just have to remember where it came from and why it's here, and *who* we have to thank."

CHAPTER 11

"The people sure are friendly here," Melissa said to Katherine after they left the art gallery and continued on their tour.

"And the buildings are so beautiful," Elise said, joining in their conversation.

"The streets are so clean and the only noises you hear are music, voices and the sound of people working. It's so different from back home," Richard added. "It makes me want to quit my job and come to live here permanently."

"I was thinking the same thing earlier," Melissa said. "The City of Love is so peaceful. I don't feel the same pressures here that I feel at home. If you developed your own talents here, people would appreciate them."

Haddi was silent during this exchange. He simply smiled enigmatically and continued walking.

"I just wish I could enjoy it more," Melissa complained. "My neck still hurts from sleeping wrong last night, and the reflection off the walls is so bright that I can barely see."

"I suppose you would get used to it if you lived here," Mary commented.

Suddenly Melissa became curious about Haddi. "Do you live here, Haddi?" she asked him. "I've certainly never seen you around Seaside before."

"No, I don't live in the City of Love," Haddi told her. "The City of Love lives within me. Will you excuse me a moment?" he added without further explanation as they came to a brick archway. Beyond it was a lush garden and beyond the trees and foliage Melissa could just make out the golden dome of a temple. Before anyone could say a word, Haddi disappeared inside.

Melissa gazed after him into the garden. "I've never seen so many beautiful plants and flowers as I have since we came on this trip. My mom has a greenhouse, but the orchids and begonias are nothing compared to the flowers in the Garden of Knowledge – and now this," she said.

"This really would be a fantastic place to live," Richard said. "It seems so removed from the rest of the world, so safe and serene. I'll bet no one even has a television here. The news of the world, the wars and plagues and petty politics, never reaches them here."

"I'm not sure whether that's good or bad," Katherine remarked thoughtfully as they continued gazing into the garden, waiting for Haddi to return.

"What do you mean?" Melissa asked. At that moment she couldn't imagine anything more comforting or enriching than living in the City of Love.

"What I mean is, it's easy to do what you're supposed to, to follow the laws of God, in a city where everyone follows the laws. You don't have to think about being trustworthy or honest or steadfast or chaste, because those virtues are common practice here."

"I think creating a spiritual society begins with each one of us," Mary mentioned. "Each of us must be kind to others, must strive to develop God's attributes like steadfastness, empathy and a prayerful attitude. You can't change society without first transforming your individual character."

"Good point. I guess if you're never tested, you'll never grow, will you?" Melissa commented. "It's that whole spiritual growth thing again, isn't it. In the last valley we learned patience by searching." She rubbed her neck and tried to stretch the kinks out of her sore back. "What's the lesson in the Valley of Love? How to endure pain?"

Katherine looked up to the tops of the highest trees in the garden and pointed to a huge nest. "The Eagle of Love has sharp claws. If there is no pain, this journey will never end. To know love truly, I've found I must endure the sadness along with the happiness, the pain with the pleasure."

"You're talking in riddles, Katherine," Elise said. "Just like Haddi does."

"I know, I'm sorry. This city makes me wax poetical. I guess what I'm trying to say is that I've found that I'm a better person for learning to live in the real world where there's pain and sorrow as well as joy. What I do is try to detach myself from the bad stuff and teach the love of God to those who will listen. Eventually everyone will begin to see the value of letting God into their lives and the whole world will become like the City of Love."

"Kind of like the Kingdom of God on earth," Elise mused. "I think I see what you mean. If we hide here in the City of Love, the problems of the world won't solve themselves and if the world falls apart, everything, including the City of Love, goes with it."

Haddi walked up just as Elise finished speaking. "It's still good to get away from it all and commune with God on a one-to-one basis. Wanting a break from the world isn't necessarily hiding," he said. "All of the Manifestations of God have done that to cleanse themselves before proclaiming their revelation. They became true lovers of God."

"Lovers?" Mary asked. "But God is an unknowable essence."

"It is true that God is unknowable and that every attempt we make to explain Him falls far short of His glory, but we can know something of God even in this physical world," Haddi continued. "We can see the signs of God all around us, in the world of nature, in the hearts of those who love Him, in the lives and teachings of His Manifestations, and in the Words of God they bring to us. In this way we can turn our hearts and souls to God, just as a plant turns to the sun.

"In this station the lover hath no thought save the Beloved, and seeketh no refuge save the Friend. At every moment he offereth a hundred lives in the path of the Loved One, at every step he throweth a thousand heads at the feet of the Beloved. But there is more than one type of love. There is the love of God for mankind, the love of mankind for God, and the love of people for each other. In each, the feeling of love is similar and does not depend on a physical presence."

"Love is eternal. I believe that," Richard said. "When you love someone, whether it is your parents, your wife, your children or a friend, it doesn't matter whether they are alive or have passed on, the love is still there."

"The love doesn't disappear after you have passed onto the next world either," Haddi said. "It is hard to understand, but because we won't have an existence in the next world as we know it in this one, the feelings we have for people and the relationships we have with them will remain with us eternally. For that reason a lover feareth nothing and no harm can come nigh him. Love is a very powerful emotion and one that will help us progress continually toward our reunion with God."

Melissa shook her head to clear it. Haddi talked about other worlds of God as if the universe were made up of a bunch of occupied planets and when people died they were just magically transported to an existence on another world. She wondered what Dobson thought about God and becoming a lover of God by serving Him. Love is eternal, her mind kept repeating. If that was true, and she married Dobson, then he might be trying to run her life for centuries, eons, millenniums. Wow!

Before she had a chance to question him further, Haddi led the way to the temple through the trees. For a moment, under the lush foliage, she felt a measure of relief from the glare and the soaring temperatures, but that moment was short-lived. The path they took curved only twice and then they emerged into an adobe courtyard, its mud-brick patio baked hard and white by the sun. Immediately she squinted against the brightness and tried to focus on the door Haddi was pointing to.

"As a special part of our tour, we'll all go into the Temple of Egypt now and sit by the fire of purification," Haddi was saying.

"Fire?" Melissa cried, peering around him into the interior of the temple. "On a hot day like this?"

She couldn't believe what she was seeing. Inside the temple a roaring fire blazed on an open hearth and sitting on benches around it were people. They were sitting so close that they almost touched the flames.

"*Until thou burn with the fire of love, thou shalt never commune with the Lover of Longing*," Haddi replied.

What did that mean? Melissa was totally confused. Why would Haddi want them to go into that temple and sit by that awful fire? The more she thought about it and struggled to understand the meaning behind his words, the worse she felt. The sun felt like an electric blanket on high beating down on her head. The heat caused her vision to blur even further and perspiration dripped down the sides of her face and into her eyes, stinging them. She raised her hand to wipe the sweat away and her back gave a nasty twinge.

"I need a shower," she declared. "I hurt all over, I'm hot and tired, I can barely see. I certainly don't want to go into that sweatbox."

"*Until, like Jacob, thou forsake thine outward eyes, thou shalt never open the eye of thine inward being*," Haddi commented.

"I don't know what you mean," Melissa said in exasperation. "You're talking in riddles again." She turned away to the left – the only way she could turn her stiff neck – and her impaired gaze fell on a sparkling, blue lake just beyond the trees surrounding the temple. Suddenly Melissa felt the overpowering urge to disobey the guide. The lake was so inviting, it just begged her to dive in.

"Look, Haddi," Melissa said. "I don't want to disappoint you, but I just know I'll die from the heat if I go into that temple and sit by that fire. Then I'll never make it on the rest of the journey to Mount Eternity. I'll just go over by the lake and wait for you there."

"You're free to choose," Haddi told her gently. "Would anyone else like to join Melissa at the lake?"

"Maybe after we sweat for a while," Richard said as he ducked his head and entered the temple. Mary followed him with a shrug and a smile and Elise and Haddi went in afterward.

"It's a hundred degrees out here and must be twice that inside," Melissa remarked to Katherine. "Are you sure you wouldn't like to go swimming with me?"

"Maybe later," Katherine said. "You really should try the fire of purification. Appearances aren't always what they seem in the City of Love."

"You guys are always saying that, but I know the difference between burning up by a fire and cooling off in a lake."

"You're welcome to join us at any time," Katherine said. "I'll see you later."

Melissa was left alone at the door of the temple, staring after her friends, whom she could only imagine were acting so irrationally because they were already suffering from heat stroke. She shook her head and wandered over toward the lake, its crystal blue waters sparkling irresistibly.

She dropped her backpack on the shore and hurried to take off her shoes. She stripped down to her shorts and tank top, which she wore under her hiking clothes, and skipped down to the water line.

"This is the next best thing to taking a shower," she said aloud, though there was no one there to hear her. Momentarily she wondered why the town's people weren't flocking to the lake on a hot day like this. "Oh, well, I have the lake all to myself."

She thought about diving straight in, but decided that she didn't know what the bottom was like and she didn't want to bruise herself on hidden rocks. Instead, she would wade out until the water was at waist level and them swim around until she had cooled off and felt refreshed. Just the thought of plunging into the clear, blue depths was exhilarating.

She curled her toes on the warm, steamy sand at the water's edge, delaying her moment of ecstacy a moment longer as she watched tiny bubbles in the lake rise and break on the surface. Then she lifted her foot and stepped into the water.

"Ouch!" she yelled and pulled her foot back immediately. "It's hot!"

She tried again with the other foot, this time stretching a little farther out thinking that the edges were heated from the sun.

"Double ouch!" she cried, jerking her foot back. The water was even hotter as it got deeper. This was strange. The day wasn't that hot. Besides, Melissa had swum in water that was as warm as taking a bath, but this water was more like boiling. She bent down and looked more closely at the bubbles.

It *was* boiling! This wasn't a lake, she realized. It was a hot spring: a giant, crystal clear, boiling, hot spring. And she had almost dived in first and checked afterward!

Just to make one last experiment, she dipped the corner of her tank top into the water. When she lifted it out, it was steaming and dried instantly. Why hadn't Haddi told her? Why hadn't Katherine warned her? She sat down on the sand and tried to puzzle it out. Lately she felt that she did nothing else except try to figure things out.

She sat down on the sand and stared out over the beautiful lake that was definitely not what it seemed. Her eyes still hurt and she was convinced that had she been able to see better, she would have noticed the steam rising off the surface of the water, and she would have paid attention to the fact that no one else frolicked in the boiling water.

Melissa curled her arms around her legs and let her head fall forward until her forehead was resting on her knees. Her neck still pained her dreadfully, but she welcomed it, because each throb brought her closer to the revelation she was seeking. Each agonizing twist of muscle made her realize that she was trying too hard to fight the inevitable.

She swiveled around and looked back down the path toward the Temple of Egypt. She could see its white walls glistening through the trees, but somehow the brightness didn't bother her as much as it had before.

She stood up, knowing that she must act, knowing that she must sacrifice her own will and enter the temple to sit by the fire of purification. Slowly she made her way back to the temple and ducked under the same doorway that her friends had walked through earlier.

Immediately the heat hit her. It was as if the waves of heat were a physical force, pushing her back, taking her breath away, making her feel faint. In the center of the room, the flames licked toward the ceiling and Melissa felt that they were already burning her, sapping her strength.

How could the others bear to sit so close? Yet, as her eyes adjusted to the interior light, she saw that they sat on benches almost touching the flames and they were laughing and talking as though the heat didn't bother them at all. And, for a brief instant, Melissa didn't think about the heat either, because she realized that her eyes didn't hurt her inside the temple. She could see perfectly.

She was about to expire from the heat, but at least she would be able to see the floor as it came up to meet her face.

Katherine motioned to her from a seat in the front row. Melissa took a deep breath and forced herself to brave the undulating waves of heat as she made her way forward. The air sizzled and cracked around her and she wondered why the entire temple didn't burst into flames.

"I'm glad you decided to come in," Katherine said as she approached.

"I don't know how long I'll be able to stay in here," Melissa said. "I can barely breathe."

"Relax. Let the fire do its job."

"I'll try to think cool thoughts," Melissa quipped and found herself able to smile slightly.

She closed her eyes and thought of rivers, mountain lakes, oceans. She tried to empty her mind of all thoughts of running away, back to her home, where things were logical. She took slow, deep breaths and tried to let go of all of her worries with each exhalation. Beads of sweat popped out all over her arms, legs and face, but she didn't touch them or wipe them away.

Suddenly a wonderful feeling came over her. Though the room was just as hot, and she could feel her perspiration soaking through her clothes, she no longer felt as uncomfortable. It was as if she was being totally drained of her worries and woes. She felt as though she was becoming clean from the inside out, purified, her inner turmoil and mortal defects washing away with the cleansing heat of the fire of purification.

Best of all, the pains in her neck and back seemed magically to disappear. And her eyes – it was incredible, but the brightness of the fire didn't bother them. She could see well again, more clearly even, than she had seen in days. It was as though a veil had been lifted, burned away by the fire of love.

Melissa found herself staring into the flames, mesmerized by the golden, flickering light. Yet the flames weren't just gold, but blue and indigo with a touch of green around the edges. The center of the fire drew her attention. There the fire was so hot, so brilliantly hot that the flames had no color at all.

The more she stared, the more the white light in the center seemed to call to her. She felt her mind drifting, letting go of its thoughts of hot and cold, of her need only a moment ago for a shower. Instead she imagined herself dissolving into the light.

Down, down she flowed, past images of events from her past, times when she had lacked compassion, had said the wrong thing, or gone along with the crowd even though she knew in her heart that it wasn't the right thing to do.

She found that while she stared into the fire, the images had no power to hurt her or make her feel guilty. When she looked away, her thoughts threatened to burn her up. It was as if the light was calling to her, urging her to give over her will to God's will, offering her peace. She forgot about the heat and the temple and her friends as she continued to stare at the light.

Was it her imagination? No, it was more than that. She couldn't have made up the overwhelming feeling of being forgiven and starting fresh. Why fight it? she thought. Why try to analyze something that couldn't be analyzed? Haddi had said that God was impossible to explain, yet she knew without a doubt in that moment that God existed and had asked her to trust in Him, to submit her will to His and allow Him to guide her.

"Oh God," Melissa whispered aloud. "I am yours to do with as you will."

Suddenly a cool breeze washed over her, despite the fire's proximity. "Come," Haddi said, beckoning them toward the door. "We must depart."

With one last look at the roaring blaze, Melissa followed the others to the back door of the temple. They stopped under a huge portal to quench their thirst at a crystal-clear fountain.

No matter how much Melissa drank she felt that she still needed more. She wasn't sure whether it was the heat from the fire which had drained the liquids in her body, or the long tour of the city, but the water was so refreshing, so pure and sweet, that she felt she could drink for ever.

Finally she looked above her head at the portal which was carved in the shape of an eagle. Its beak was open, intent on its next victim, claws extended down the sides of the door frame, frozen in flight.

Melissa shuddered.

Katherine noticed and came to stand by her. The two girls studied the intricately carved doorway together. "The Eagle of Love," Katherine said, answering Melissa's unspoken question. "It's symbolic of the way love grabs you and won't let you go."

"It's not bad to be caught by love," Melissa mused. "Before I came into the temple I had a lot of doubts about myself, but sitting by the fire seemed to put everything into perspective. I keep wondering, if I sat by the fire of love every day, would I eventually know all of the answers to my questions?"

"The next valley is the Valley of Knowledge,"

Katherine said. "We must escape the claws of the Eagle of Love first, then maybe you can leave your doubts behind and move into certitude."

"How long will it take to get to the Valley of Knowledge?" Melissa asked as they passed together under the eagle portal, carefully avoiding the sharp, outstretched claws.

"Not long at all," Katherine said with a grin. She waved her hand at the panoramic view in front of them.

"This is it?" Melissa asked, staring. Before them stretched a wide, flat meadow filled with wild flowers and grazing deer. She looked back through the portal, past the fire and through the front door of the temple. She could still see the City of Love framed in the opening. "Incredible! I never would have guessed that it was so close."

"Sometimes the valleys are as close as a heartbeat," Katherine said.

"Amazing," Melissa remarked, looking around. "Truly amazing."

CHAPTER 12

"It's beautiful," Melissa breathed. "Just like a painting."

"Aren't you going to ask how long it will take us to get through this valley?" Katherine teased.

Melissa shook her head as she strapped her backpack more tightly around her waist and tightened the shoulder straps to prepare for the hike ahead of them.

"It's funny," she said. "There was something about sitting at the fire of purification that made me realize that I'm always too worried about the result and that I don't take time to enjoy the process. I guess the Valley of Search taught me that, too, but sitting by the fire and forcing myself to let go of my doubts made things very clear."

"How so?"

"Well, for one thing, I'm on this trip because *I* want to be. Not because I'm proving something to Dobson, or because my parents want to be able to tell all of their friends how brave their daughter is. It's me. I'm the one who wants to make the journey. I'm the one who wants to find out more about myself and where I'm going with my life. If I rush through it as fast as I can, I won't be able to do that."

Melissa fell into step behind the others and Katherine

paced along beside her.

"What happened to you when you came on this journey the first time?" Melissa asked.

"I was really scared," Katherine remarked. "I was a real basket case in the Valley of Search and I did more than just stick my toe in the burning lake. I burned my whole leg!"

"Really? Why didn't you warn me? No, forget that," she said quickly. "I know that I had to find out for myself."

They walked along in silence for a moment, each girl contemplating her own reality and drinking in the sights and sounds of the meadow filled with wildlife. Butterflies danced on wisps of sunlight, sparrows chirped, flying and diving in the air currents, while rabbits hopped shyly from flower to flower. Melissa was certain that no camera could do justice to the serenity of the Valley of Knowledge, that no description would be adequate.

Then they topped a small rise and directly in front of them was a gate. The large, stone portico had sculptured wrought iron across its center, but was attached to no fence on either side. It stood effortlessly in the center of the meadow, beckoning the travelers with the certain knowledge that they must pass through it to continue on their journey.

"What's that?" Elise asked.

"The Gate of Truth and Piety," Haddi replied.

No longer doubting the wisdom of their guide, Melissa stepped forward. "Do we go through it?" she asked.

"Certainly," Haddi said. "Every wayfarer on this journey must set ajar the Gate of Truth and Piety and shut the doors of vain imaginings. He or she must be content with the decree of God."

"What if we don't know what that decree is?" Mary asked.

"We must be content with whatever has gone before and whatever will pass in the future because that is the secret of everlasting life," Haddi explained. "In war, there is peace; in death, life; in ignorance, knowledge is hidden; and in knowledge, a myriad wisdoms manifest."

"I'm not sure I understand," Richard remarked.

"Me neither," Melissa said.

"Maybe it's not necessary to understand everything completely," Elise commented. "Sometimes the reasons become clear later on."

"Why don't we pause for a moment of prayer before we pass through the gate," Haddi suggested.

Everyone stopped and this time, instead of thinking other thoughts, Melissa let the words of the prayer flow around her, and opened her mind to the possibilities.

"*Make firm our steps, O Lord, in Thy path and strengthen Thou our hearts in Thine obedience. Turn our faces toward the beauty of Thy oneness and gladden our bosoms with the signs of Thy divine unity. Adorn our bodies with the robe of Thy bounty, and remove from our eyes the veil of sinfulness, and give us the chalice of Thy grace; that the essence of all beings may sing Thy praise before the vision of Thy grandeur. Reveal then Thyself, O Lord, by Thy merciful utterance and the mystery of Thy divine being, that the holy ecstasy of prayer may fill our souls – a prayer that shall rise above words and letters and transcend the murmur of syllables and sounds – that all things may be merged into nothingness before the revelation of Thy splendor.*"

When Haddi finished chanting, the air around Melissa seemed to be vibrating with a power and energy all its own. Was this God? Wouldn't it be simpler if God just appeared, in the flesh, and told her in no uncertain terms what she needed to do with her life?

Here she was, about to go through the Gate of Truth and Piety, and she was about the most unsure, confused person in the world.

Why would God want her anyway? She wasn't even close to being saintly. Although she had previously thought of herself as a decent person – she did volunteer work for charities, she tried to be nice to her friends, she didn't cheat on her homework – there had been plenty of times when she had bent the rules to suit her own needs.

Flashes of memory assailed her as she walked slowly toward the gate. What was truth? Was it absolute honesty? If so, then she hadn't been honest with Dobson when she told him why she wanted to go on this trip. She had been afraid to discuss her true worries about feeling suppressed and taken advantage of, about feeling out of control and anxious about her life beyond high school. At the time, she had convinced herself that she was trying to protect him, to avoid hurting his feelings. Really, though, she had been protecting herself, afraid to take the chance of causing an argument, or even worse, risk being rejected.

And what about that time she let her friends convince her to ditch school last fall? She had told her teacher that she had to go to the next town to visit a sick relative. She hadn't exactly *lied*. She *did* stop by Great-aunt Myrtle's nursing home and take her a bouquet of flowers and a basket of yarn, but the rest of the day, she and Dobson and several others had driven the back roads of the state of Washington, glorying in their escape from school.

Suddenly Melissa felt very unworthy. Who was she to even step one foot through the Gate of Truth and Piety? She wasn't nearly good enough.

"Katherine, I don't know about this," Melissa said, hesitating. "Suddenly I feel so weak and lowly, so selfish and self-centered. I'm not the least bit brave about facing my true self. Can't we just walk around it and avoid the whole issue?"

Katherine stopped and gazed with Melissa at the imposing gate in front of them. "No one is perfect," she said quietly. "Life is a process of making day-to-day choices. Remember the Valley of Search, where finding the way out wasn't as important as the search itself."

"I know. I thought I understood that. But this truth thing . . . I mean, I know this is just a heap of stones and iron, but the thought of truth and piety makes me wonder about all of God's attributes that Haddi was telling us people could mirror – trustworthiness, loyalty, steadfastness, severance, detachment . . . If I can't even accomplish *one* attribute like honesty, how will I ever be ready to take on the rest?"

Haddi walked up to them then. He put his hand on Melissa's shoulder, but he addressed the rest of the group as well as her. "The limitations we feel are of our own making. Remember the fire of purification? God sees us all as perfect. Everyone is traveling the same path, we're just at different stages. However, no one walking the path may look down on another or try to put himself or herself above someone else. Only God may judge. Fear God, and you need not fear anyone or anything else."

The words 'fear God' and 'judgment' propelled her forward with thoughts of retribution, yet she had felt only love on this journey. She thought about the tablet

she had found by the Tree of Being that had told her to 'Fear God, and God will give you knowledge.' Perhaps fear and judgment had more to do with respect and justice than punishments. In any case, each day was a new beginning, each step a chance to grow in her knowledge of herself and God, each moment left behind all the other moments that might not have been as good as she wanted, but were, nevertheless, learning experiences.

With less trepidation than she had felt a moment before, she squared her shoulders and marched through the gate, emerging once again into the same meadow beyond. Somehow, though, the grass and trees and flowers looked different to her, more distinct, clearer. How could passing through the Gate of Truth and Piety, isolated in the center of the Valley of Knowledge, have changed her perceptions so greatly? She wasn't sure, but when she looked back as the iron gate swung closed, she knew that it had.

For the rest of the afternoon the group made good time through the fertile valley. The meadow grasses were soft and the ground beneath spongy and resilient to their tired feet. Melissa felt her aches and pains completely vanish as she walked with a measured gait. Compared to the steep descent into the Valley of Search and the rocky pass into the Valley of Love, the Valley of Knowledge was a breeze.

Dusk fell and Haddi signaled for them to halt. "We will rest here for the night and enter the Valley of Unity at dawn."

"How far is it?" Elise asked.

"Not far," Haddi replied.

Melissa and Katherine began to help set up camp. Melissa gathered stones and wood for the fire while

Katherine shook out their groundsheets and sleeping bags.

It was peaceful in the Valley of Knowledge. Melissa felt more content than she had since the trip began. She welcomed the darkness and pushed aside all thoughts about how far they had come or how far they had yet to go. Even though it seemed that they would need all seven days at this rate just to reach Mount Eternity, Melissa trusted Haddi. If he said they could go the distance and return in one week, then it must be so.

And what was the worst that could happen? She'd be late for school on Monday morning. Her parents would worry, but would Dobson? He would probably waste no time in telling everyone that he had warned her against going, that he had tried to stop her. He would get a lot of mileage out of her disappearance, being the grieving boyfriend and all. And then, when she did return, he would get even more mileage out of the guilt he would heap on her.

"You're scowling, Melissa," Katherine said. "Is something troubling you?"

"I was thinking about Dobson. I've been thinking about him a lot since I've been on this trip," Melissa told her.

"Do you miss him?"

"Actually, no. I find myself wondering about our relationship, if you could call it that. The longer I'm away from him the more I realize how stifling it has become. Either subtly, or blatantly, he runs my life. I don't think I want him to do that any more."

"I'm sure you'll figure out what's right for you," Katherine said. "Sometimes making changes is hard, but the results are worth it, especially in the way you feel

113

about yourself."

As they were speaking, Haddi took several battery-operated lanterns out of his pack. He turned them on, one by one, as the darkness grew, until the group was working around the fire in a circle of light. Beyond the circle the night shadows deepened and closed in, but they were friendly shadows.

Melissa felt the tendrils of darkness almost tangibly and their all-encompassing blackness comforted her as she loaded her tin plate with stew and dumplings.

There wasn't much small talk during the meal. It was as though everyone was digesting all that they had seen and heard and experienced along with the food.

Finally Haddi set aside his plate and leaned forward. "What do you think of this valley?" he asked the group.

Elise was the first to speak. "This is, by far, the most beautiful place I have ever seen."

"No defect canst thou see in the creation of the God of Mercy," Haddi said. "There isn't a single flaw."

"It's hard to believe after walking as long as we walked, but my feet and back feel better now than they did when we started out," Richard commented. "The ground itself gives you strength."

"I feel the same way," Melissa said. "I can't really remember the beginning of the journey and I'm not thinking about the end because there's so much peace and contentment here."

Haddi nodded in understanding. "This is a good place, and a good time, to talk about the Glory of God and His message for this day."

Melissa settled back to listen, bracing herself on one elbow. This time when Haddi spoke, she intended to really pay attention and learn.

"God has always been and will always be," Haddi told them. "He has never left mankind alone. Through His Manifestations – some religions call them Prophets – God renews His teachings in each age, bringing wisdom for those who are ready to accept it."

"What wisdom has God brought for this age?" Mary asked curiously. "I know one thing. Coming on this trip has made me realize that God isn't just a book or a visit to a church on Sunday. On this journey, I feel as if God is everywhere, in everything I see and do."

"*The Wayfarer mounteth on the ladders of inner truth and hasteneth to the heaven of inner significance*," Haddi said. "God's teachings are manifest in all created things, all knowledge, all thought, all feeling. In this day the followers of God must look toward unity as the pervasive power that will bind the hearts of men."

"Does that mean that everyone should strive to be the same?" Elise asked as she sipped her tea.

"Unity does not mean sameness. It means awareness and acceptance of the diversity around us, yet we are all tied together by a common thread, a common bond. Men and women must be equal. They are not the same, shall never be the same, have different strengths and weaknesses, but God loves all unconditionally. And we must love each other the same way."

"The world has a long way to go before it reaches the point of treating men and women as equals," Melissa commented.

"Though outwardly it appears that the sexes are still struggling, the seed has been planted," Haddi said. "When the Manifestation of God appears in the world, the energy of His revelation permeates everything. Just as in its seed is hidden the mighty oak, in the seed of disunity is the flower of unity."

"How is that possible?" Richard asked. "I don't see anything unifying about disunity."

"I think I understand," Melissa said. "Take war, for instance. If the fighting gets bad enough, more and more people lose their lives, and eventually those involved begin to realize that there *must* be a better way."

"That's true," Richard admitted. "There have been more peace talks and disarmament agreements in recent history than ever before."

"I've always thought that the whole world is connected," Mary added. "It's time people realized how much their actions affect others."

"We still have a long way to go before the world could be considered unified," Elise said. "Just wanting it isn't enough. We have to *do* something to make unity happen."

Mary leaned forward. "What else can we do, Haddi?" she prompted.

"Science and religion must be in harmony. Their essential foundation is the same. Likewise, all people must adopt a common language, a common monetary system and must promote universal education. This is not to deny that which already exists, because all people should be proud of their heritage. But, for the peoples of the world to move forward into the Most Great Peace, they must be able to speak to each other, to trade equally, and to interact with each other intelligently. The Manifestation of God for this day has said it must be so."

"This all sounds wonderful," Melissa said, "but how will people know of this Manifestation?"

Haddi smiled. "They must seek."

Melissa attempted to digest this last bit of

information. Did that mean that people would come from all over the world to climb Mount Eternity? Or were there other journeys, other valleys? And what would happen once she reached the summit? Would she go back to her old life, exactly as it was before? Would Mount Eternity, and her adventure getting there, fade to only a pleasant memory?

"I like to think of religion as a way of life," Elise said. "It's not just saying a prayer, it's *living* the prayer."

"It's not just talking about making a change, it's really changing," added Katherine. "Religion, to me, is working every day to know and to love God and through acquiring His attributes, improve both myself and the world around me."

Haddi stirred the fire and the embers glowed with new life. "When a person accepts the station of the Lord, they will no longer wander in the darkness of illusion, nor need lamps to guide them. They will quench the lamps because the sun has risen and they will have assistance from holy souls."

CHAPTER 13

Tired from their eventful day, Melissa and Katherine retired early, and were lulled to sleep by the crackling of the fire and the murmur of voices still talking things out, sifting through their experiences.

At first Melissa's sleep seemed dreamless. Her consciousness, completely relaxed, floated in a sea of comforting blackness, much the same as the shadows that had surrounded their camp as night fell. She drifted along, oblivious, without a care.

Then in her hand, a lamp appeared – not a battery-operated lantern, but the old-fashioned kind, with a wick and a smoking flame. In the blackness she held it up, but the light barely illumined her own hand and arm, much less the darkness around her, or the gravel that suddenly crunched beneath her feet.

Then, in the distance, she spotted another pinprick of light, another traveler perhaps. She half-floated, half-walked toward the light, which became bigger and brighter as she neared it. The closer she got, the more things came into focus. First she saw only herself, then the ground she was walking on and finally, the trees and clouds overhead. The light she had been walking toward had been the sun cresting over the eastern horizon, bathing the day with its glory.

From the center of the light, a man appeared. He, too, glowed brilliantly, his light-colored clothing reflecting the dawn's early rays.

The man beckoned to her and she walked toward his outstretched hand. She gazed into his eyes and imagined that she saw the entire universe with all its magical mysteries. She wasn't afraid, not even when she realized that her feet were no longer touching the earth. She simply allowed herself to float alongside the shining man; up, up into the sky, far above the world, until the whole, blue, green and white ball was visible, just as it is for the astronauts from space.

She imagined that God saw the world this way, pure and unified. From this height there were no boundaries, no shades of prejudice, no questions of equality. It was obvious that the world, and everyone and everything that lived on it, were one creation.

She turned her head to gaze at her companion and saw to her amazement that great, silver wings flowed from his back, and circled round her, protecting her and holding her up. She thought about speaking to him, but there didn't seem a need.

To Melissa, her mind seemed full of sounds, which didn't need words for interpretation. Below, from the earth, a cacophony of rhythms assailed her – the crash of the ocean's waves, the crescendo of a symphony orchestra, the murmur of billions of voices, dogs barking, babies laughing, birds singing.

Beyond them, the planets whirred around the sun, and beyond the solar system, a thousand suns, a million planets danced, while asteroids whizzed and atmospheric clouds billowed.

The shining man slowly rotated, facing her toward the sun, but instead of hurting her eyes, she was able to see beyond the bursting gases to the molten center. The sun's rays bathed her in warmth and light, and, as she turned her head to follow each ray with her gaze, she saw that the sun touched each tiny, infinitesimal part of God's creation equally, training it according to its potential. Name and fame and rank meant nothing in the sight of God. A pure heart and radiant acquiescence to His will meant everything.

The shining man who had lifted her to the heights of glory, slowly lowered her back down to earth. She saw the clouds, the mountaintops covered with sparkling, untouched snow, the oceans, trees and finally the meadow at the edge of the Valley of Knowledge, where all of her friends still lay sleeping.

"Thank you," she said silently, and her mind carried the words to the shining man.

He smiled, a beautiful, heartwarming, all-accepting smile. Then he spoke, and his melodious voice seemed to speak directly to her soul. "*Verily, we are from God and to Him shall we return.*"

Melissa lay down on her sleeping bag with her eyes open, intending to watch the shining man ascend into the heavens, but instead he reached out softly and brushed the feather-light tips of his wing across her eyes.

She slept and woke with a song of praise on her lips.

"*O God! Refresh and gladden my spirit. Purify my heart. Illumine my powers. I lay all my affairs in Thy hand. I will no longer be sorrowful and grieved. I will be a happy and joyful being. I will no longer be full of anxiety, nor will I let trouble harass me. I will not dwell on the unpleasant things of life. O God! Thou art more friend to me than I am to myself.*

I dedicate myself to Thee, O Lord."

She hadn't realized that she was singing aloud until she opened her eyes and found the rest of the group looking at her. It wasn't yet dawn, and the meadow around them was bathed in a grayish half-light, not yet day, no longer night.

"That was beautiful," Elise told her. "You have a wonderful singing voice. Have you taken lessons?"

"No," Melissa told her. "Until this moment I didn't even know those words, or the tune. I've never really sung much before. But, today, this valley makes me feel like singing."

"Me, too," Katherine said.

They hummed as they worked together, heating the water for their tea and re-rolling their sleeping bags.

"I feel as though I've finally left the rest of my world behind. I'm thinking only about the present and the journey ahead. I'm thinking constantly about how I can become a better person, and in turn, make the world a better place to live in. I can work on becoming more honest, more creative, more respectful, more responsible, more enthusiastic. Does that sound hopelessly idealistic and foolish?"

"Not at all," Katherine said. "Your heart has become pure and free from limitations. Your vision is no longer blinded by self and passion. The Valley of Knowledge is the last plane of limitation. From now on, we soar!"

"Last week I wouldn't have believed that," Melissa said, remembering her precious dream and the sensation of flying. "But, from now on, I'll believe anything. This journey has made me realize that anything is possible."

A few moments later the wayfarers gathered around the fire as had become their custom. Haddi greeted each with a hug. "Welcome to the Valley of Unity," he said.

"Pardon me?" Richard asked. "I thought we were in the Valley of Knowledge."

"The Valley of Knowledge and the Valley of Unity are but a breath apart. Here," he said, holding out a dipper full of tea and filling Richard's cup to the brim. He dipped out equal portions from the pot of tea and filled each of their cups in turn. "Drink from the cup of the Absolute and gaze on the Manifestations of Oneness. God is one, there is none other God but He. And, His Manifestations are one, even though they appear in different personages, at different ages of mankind's maturity, and bring what appears to be different revelations."

"If all of the Manifestations of God are one, and have the same knowledge, the knowledge of God," Elise asked, "why didn't the first one reveal it all? Then there would be no need for others and all the confusion it causes to the followers of the previous religion."

"The Manifestations of God are like schoolteachers. Though they are all trained by the all-knowing hand of God, and are all endowed with the same attributes, they must adapt their presentations of God's all-encompassing will to the people of the age in which they appear. As humanity's understanding grows, so too do the complexities of God's revelations."

"In other words, more is revealed as people mature spiritually," Melissa said, amazed at herself for understanding so quickly.

"Yes," Haddi agreed. "A first-grade teacher receives the same education as a sixth-grade teacher, but she would not teach sixth-grade concepts to her seven-year-olds. She would prepare them gradually."

"First things first," Mary said. "You must crawl before you walk."

"And now, we must walk," Haddi remarked. "The Sea of Spirit is only a mile or so. We can be there by dawn and watch the sunrise."

Everyone picked up a lantern and turned it on. They fell into step, one behind the other, and struck off across the meadow toward the lightening sky.

All around her, Melissa watched the meadow come alive. Though she knew she was awake, she still held onto the remnants of her dream. She remembered what the world looked like from far out in space and tried to see it with the same oneness that she had felt, cradled in the wings of the shining man. Truly, even from this earthly vantage point, she could see no imperfections, no divisions, only unity. She wondered whether everyone else had experienced a dream about unity also, and if that was why they were all in the Valley of Unity now.

Before she realized that they had walked the mile, the group was standing on the shore of a slick, crystal blue lake.

"The Sea of Spirit," Haddi announced.

"It's so glassy, just like a mirror," Mary said. "I can see myself."

Melissa walked to the edge of the sea and bent to see her reflection. She was amazed by what she saw. Where her brow had been almost permanently furrowed back home, now her forehead was free from worry wrinkles. Her chestnut hair framed her face in abandoned disarray, giving her the appearance of a wild, free, woodland sprite. Was it a trick of the morning light on the water that made her features appear to glow radiantly, or had something fundamental inside her changed?

She splashed a little water on her face and waited for the ripples to clear before gazing into the water again.

"I look so different," she exclaimed. "I hardly know it's me." She took off her shoes and waded into the cool water.

Katherine followed her example and they splashed each other like children. Melissa had never felt so free.

"Your heart has become pure and it reflects the attributes of God," Haddi said from beside her. "You have recognized the Messenger of God for this day, have flown with Him to the heights of spiritual ecstacy, have seen the world and all therein with a new eye, heard with a new ear."

"My dream!" Melissa exclaimed as she stepped out of the water and dried her feet. "How do you know about my dream? Is the shining man the Messenger?" she asked as she put on her shoes.

Haddi smiled. "I did not know that you dreamt. I only knew that your joy of discovery is apparent on your face. Truly, for you, the sun has risen."

Melissa looked to the east where the golden globe of the sun was just bulging over the horizon. Of course the sun had risen, she thought. Wasn't it obvious? Hadn't it risen for everyone?

Melissa switched off her lantern and turned toward the sun, letting its dawning warmth seep into her. She closed her eyes and felt tiny tingles all along her body as the sun reached first her face, then her hands, and then warmed its way through her clothing to heat all of her.

When she opened her eyes she realized that there were more people than just her group at the Sea of Spirit. Several others wandered, stumbled really, around the shores of the lake. Their tarnished lanterns and old flashlights were still lit and they peered into the daylight as if it was still dark.

"Pardon me," one man said, bumping into Melissa. "Can you show me the way to the Sea of Spirit? I know it's around here somewhere."

"Why, it's right here, only a few feet away," Melissa said, pointing to the lake.

The man held up his lantern and peered into the distance, unseeing. "Where?" he asked again.

"Right here," Melissa said kindly. "You may turn off your lamp now. The sun has risen. Don't you see it?"

The man shook his head as if she were deluded. "I've been searching too long to listen to tall stories," he said. "I'll find it myself!"

"But . . . " Melissa began uncertainly. Couldn't he see the lake? Couldn't he see that it was already daylight? Maybe it had to do with recognizing the Messenger.

Melissa approached a woman who was bending down and shining her lamp in the dust. "The sun has risen," Melissa told her. "Have you heard that God has sent a new Messenger? He has come to show us the way toward unity. All Manifestations of God are one, all people are one, men and women are equal, science and religion must be in harmony, everyone must be educated . . . "

Her voice trailed off. The woman wasn't even listening. She was humming to herself and sifting the dust beneath her feet, holding each granule up to the light.

"What is she looking for?" Melissa asked Katherine. "Why can't these people see that it's daytime?"

Katherine studied the woman for a moment. "Even though she stands in the Valley of Unity, her heart is still in the Valley of Search. She'll find the lake, but she must find it on her own. Come on. We have a lot of ground to cover."

Melissa hated to leave the people behind. She wished that there was some way she could share her dream with them and help them on their search. They clung so desperately to their old, tarnished lamps. She wondered if that was what Haddi had meant when he explained that the Manifestations of God were the light and the lamp was only the outer covering – the laws and tenets of religion for the day in which the Messenger appeared. She remembered him saying that people became attached to the lamps and couldn't see the same light when it reappeared in a new lamp. Maybe it was easier for her, because she hadn't really been attached to any particular religion before coming on this trip.

Hiking along with the others, they followed the shoreline for a while, then struck off cross country. Their path gradually climbed uphill, sloping gently toward the distant mountains. It was remarkably free from vegetation, almost desert-like, as they hiked through the heat of the morning and into the afternoon.

Yet, even in the desolation, there was beauty. Melissa ceased wondering about the climate and terrain changes that had marked their journey and concentrated instead on keeping her pace steady and her breathing even as the climb grew steeper.

Finally, midway through the afternoon, Haddi called a halt in a clearing, surrounded by pines with a beautiful view beyond into the next valley. But Melissa scarcely looked at the valley to come because, also nestled under the trees on the edge of the clearing, was a tiny, one-room schoolhouse.

She knew it was a schoolhouse because it looked just

like the old-fashioned schoolhouses that she had seen pictures of in her history books at school, a perfect replica of turn-of-the-century education. She could almost imagine a strait-laced schoolmarm standing in the doorway and ringing the bell to call the children in from recess.

What was a schoolhouse doing there? Who had built it?

Melissa turned to Katherine to ask if she had seen it on her previous journeys, but the sound of the bell brought her head back around.

DONG! DONG! DONG!

The bell wasn't the most surprising thing, however. It was the person ringing it. There in the doorway, his hand on the rope, was the shining man from her dream!

CHAPTER 14

"That's him!" Melissa whispered, nudging Katherine. "That's the shining man from my dream, the one who carried me out into space so that I could see the earth without all of its man-made boundaries."

"He'll be our teacher for the rest of the afternoon," Katherine said, neither confirming nor negating Melissa's statement.

Above the entrance to the building was a hand-written sign which read, 'Schoolhouse of Oneness.'

Melissa blinked, and looked at the man again. The wings were gone, and he wasn't shining now, although she noticed as she went closer that he still seemed to glow with an unseen radiance, that an energy surrounded him, gleaming almost visibly from every limb and member. Despite these differences, however, she was sure that the man standing in the doorway of the schoolhouse and the man in her dream were one and the same.

"Melissa, Katherine, Elise, Mary, Richard," Haddi said, indicating each person in turn, "this is the *Adib-i-Eshgh*, which means the Master of Love."

"Come in and rest, before we begin the lesson for today," Master Eshgh said, his voice melodious and welcoming.

They followed him into the schoolhouse, the interior of which completely matched Melissa's expectations. In the front stood a teacher's desk, and behind it hung a large chalkboard. Benches were arranged in a circle in the center of the wood floor around a hand-hewn, block table. Bright, gingham curtains were tied back with matching bows on the windows.

Melissa couldn't stop staring at Master Eshgh. Never before had she dreamed a dream and then met the person in real life. It was amazing. Wait until she told this story to Dobson.

Dobson. She realized that it was the first time she had thought of him in over a day. She realized something else, too. Dobson would just laugh at her if she told him of her dreams, of her revelations, of her trip at all.

She watched as Master Eshgh served them freshly squeezed fruit juice in carved wooden cups and cut them slices of homemade bread. She accepted the delicacies and ate and drank with relish.

Suddenly she realized that she didn't care what Dobson thought. She wouldn't be afraid to tell him, or anyone else for that matter, about her trip. If they chose not to believe her, then that was their problem. Just because someone didn't believe it, didn't mean it wasn't all true.

It was kind of like Haddi's explanation about the existence of God. There can't be a creation without a creator, he had said. But, whether the creation believes in the creator or not, the creator still exists. The creator isn't dependent on belief.

Above all, Melissa knew that everything happening to her on this trip was true and real, perhaps the most real thing that had ever happened to her. She also knew that when she returned she would have to share her experiences, no matter what the reaction.

When everyone had been served, Master Eshgh went to the chalkboard and wrote, 'Four kinds of Love. Four Divine States.'

"Today," he said, "our lesson is about love. We will speak about the kinds of love that exist. *The journeys in the pathway of love are reckoned as four: From the creatures to the True One; from the True One to the creatures; from the creatures to the creatures; from the True One to the True One.*"

"That makes sense," Elise said. "People love God. Without their love for God, they would not follow His laws, or grow spiritually."

"And God loves people and other creatures," Mary said. "It was His love that created us in the first place so that we could come to know and to love Him."

Master Eshgh smiled and Melissa could feel his energy. Somehow she knew she should be the next one to speak.

"People must love other people. Not just your family or your friends, but everyone," she said thoughtfully. "I can see that if they love God first, then their love for each other is much more pure. They will be able to understand the essential unity that joins all things, and will be able to accept the differences as well as the similarities in others."

Richard nodded. "And just as we are supposed to love others, we are supposed to love ourselves, for without that love, we have no reason to strive, to grow."

"God also loves Himself," Katherine remarked. "That is the greatest love of all."

"If the love of God did not exist then the light of

unity could not illuminate humanity," Master Eshgh concluded.

They were in the Valley of Unity and the meaning of the word was becoming much more clear to Melissa. Each thing had its place, but each was also part of the whole. Each was necessary, yet could not survive alone.

"God is, in Himself, the embodiment of Unity," Master Eshgh said. "He is the first and the last, the Seen and the Hidden, as are all of us."

"How is that possible?" Melissa asked. "I can understand that God might have those attributes because He has ever been, will always be, can be seen through the mirrors of His Messengers and in the hearts of His followers, yet no one can actually touch His Being. But how can people attain these stations?"

"Let me give you an example, Melissa," Master Eshgh said. "You already have an excellent understanding of the divine states. Think of it this way. Each of us has a different state in relation to others. *Thou art first in relation to thy son, last in relation to thy father.*"

Melissa nodded. "What about the seen and the hidden?"

"*In thine outward appearance, thou tellest of the appearance of power in the realms of divine creation; in thine inward being thou revealest the hidden mysteries which are the divine trust deposited within thee.*"

"That's right. No one knows what goes on inside my head, yet my thoughts are just as much a part of me as my physical body."

"People can make you do things physically, but they can't control your mind," Katherine said. "For instance, you might be required to attend class, but, while you sit there, your thoughts might be far away."

"That's been happening to me a lot lately," Melissa confessed.

"True learning only comes when there is a need and a desire to learn," Haddi said.

"I've learned a lot on this trip," Melissa said.

The others echoed her sentiment with murmurs of assent.

"On this journey," Master Eshgh told them, "you must forsake the inner land of unreality for thy true station, and dwell within the shadow of the tree of knowledge. There will be many dangers, both real and imaginary, on the rest of your trip."

"What kind of dangers?" Mary asked.

"*Impoverish thyself, that thou mayest enter the high court of riches; and humble thy body, that thou mayest drink from the river of glory.* Your vision must remain as sharp as the falcon so that in every city you will behold a world, in every valley reach a spring, in every meadow hear a song. You must search your soul to distinguish truth from falsehood and be detached from the result."

As the wayfarers left the Schoolhouse of Oneness, Melissa was deep in thought. Master Eshgh had said so many things, and she knew that each one was like a drop that would explain the whole ocean, if she could only understand.

They all picked up their backpacks and shouldered them, then said their goodbyes. Melissa and Katherine walked off a little distance by themselves and turned to look back at the gorgeous landscape around them while Haddi had a final discussion with Master Eshgh.

"What did he mean by impoverish ourselves?" Melissa asked Katherine. "Get rid of all of our possessions? Give away all of our money? Live on the street? And then, if God gives us this high court of riches, do we give that away also?"

"Do you remember that I mentioned earlier the fact that God has put all of the good things on this earth that we might enjoy them? He isn't asking us to give away everything. He's asking us to become so detached that it wouldn't matter if it was gone."

"I've been really attached to things in the past. I mean, I live in a family that collects things for a living. My father places a lot of value on the objects he imports and if something breaks, he's devastated, even if it's insured.

"And I'm hooked on some other, less tangible, things," Melissa continued. "Like training and winning at track meets. In the past, I've felt a real drive to win at all costs. The coaches train us that way."

"The hardest thing to be detached from is our self-image. We get hooked on acting, dressing, talking or eating a certain way – even sleeping in a certain bed in a certain position," Katherine said. "Changing is harder if we feel we are losing something rather than gaining."

"I know what you mean. I've spent the past two years staying with Dobson, even though I don't think he is the best person for me, because I'm afraid if I lose him there won't be anyone to replace him. I'm beginning to realize that isn't true."

Katherine waved her hand at the secluded clearing. "Look," she said.

Melissa took in the beauty of the forest glen, the vision of rainbow colors of flowers, varying shades of green leaves. It was beautiful and she knew she would remember it always.

"Now, close your eyes," Katherine said. "If you were

blind, would you still enjoy this clearing?"

Melissa was silent for a moment, listening to the sound of the wind in the top needles of the pines, the call of a turtle dove, the rustle of the grass. She nodded.

"Now cover your ears," Katherine instructed.

Melissa did, and immediately she smelled the sweetest, pine-scented breeze. She felt the sun as it penetrated the leafy canopy overhead, and dappled her skin with warmth. The fresh, mountain air tasted cool and pungent on her tongue. She sensed the vibrations of the others around her.

"Now, what if you lost all of your senses? If you couldn't see, touch, hear, smell or taste? Would you still enjoy this clearing?"

Melissa kept her eyes closed and tried to find a place deep within herself that could answer that question truthfully. "Yes," she finally said. "Because the clearing is still there in my mind. Just thinking about it evokes memories and dreams, which give me the same feeling of contentment that I'm experiencing now. Is that what it means to be detached?"

"That's one of the ways that I interpret it," Katherine said. "I'm sure there are many more. I do know that the four types of love that Master Eshgh was talking about are the most important concepts to learn."

"That's true," Melissa said. "Without them, none of us, and none of this," she added, gesturing with her arm at their surroundings, "would exist."

"Shall we?" Haddi invited, gesturing to the path ahead.

Mary, Richard, Elise, Katherine and Melissa followed him along a curving forest path, deep into the trees on the far side of the clearing. They were still climbing and

Melissa wondered just how far up the next valley was.

"Our next stop is the Plain of Spirit," Haddi said, answering her unspoken question. "We will be there shortly, and from there we'll be able to see the Valley of Contentment."

"So soon?" Melissa asked. "The first few valleys seemed to have taken forever, and now I feel as if we're going too fast. I want to stay longer, put off reaching Mount Eternity, because, as soon as we get there, I know we'll have to turn around and go back."

"Detachment," Katherine said, a smile parting her lips.

"Easier said than done," Melissa said, one eyebrow raised ruefully.

Not long afterward, and much sooner than Melissa wanted, the group emerged above the tree line onto a wide, flat plateau. She knew immediately that this was the Plain of Spirit. She knew because, from their great height, all that rose above them was the sky and the misty slopes of Mount Eternity in the near distance. From the Plain of Spirit, she felt as though she was almost touching heaven.

"Where is the next valley?" Elise enquired.

Melissa walked to the edge of the plateau and looked down. Below them was the largest, and highest, inland lake she had ever seen. It stretched for miles in all directions. Jutting up from the waves were hundreds of jagged peaks, their rocky points polished white from the incessant battering of the wind.

Indeed, Melissa had to brace herself to keep from tumbling off the plateau and falling to her death on the spires below. If that was the valley, she saw no path down into it, and even if they did hike down there, they would have to swim or have a boat. And even with a boat, the high winds whipped the lake water into such a froth of waves and whitecaps that any craft trying to negotiate the hazardous rock formations would surely be crushed and broken to bits.

"It looks impassable," Melissa remarked. "What are we going to do, Haddi?"

Haddi held out his hands, palms upraised. He smiled that enigmatic little smile of his and walked over to a stack of what looked like canvases, stretched on frames. He held one up and to Melissa it resembled a giant kite.

Then, as if it was the most natural thing in the world, Haddi announced, "We're going to fly!"

CHAPTER 15

"Fly?" Melissa gulped. "With only those . . . kites?"

"The Valley of Contentment can only be traversed through the air," Haddi explained patiently. "The winds of divine contentment blow from the Plain of the Spirit and will support you as you glide over the valley."

Suddenly Melissa forgot everything that she had learned about trusting God and being detached from the world. It was one thing to talk about leaving your earthly possessions in the dust or to dream of fanciful flights above in the cosmos, but she wasn't ready to risk her life for her new Beloved. She knew for absolute certain that if she strapped one of those kite contraptions onto her back and attempted to fly over the Valley of Contentment, she would end up battered and broken on the jagged peaks below.

How could they even call this the Valley of Contentment? She was anything but content. She was frustrated. She was angry. She was frightened – make that scared to death. No one had ever asked her to face death on fabric wings. She would just turn right around and hike back the way she came. The rest of them could fly off to their doom, but Melissa would be level-headed and sensible. Four valleys were enough.

"K-k-katherine?" she stammered. "I don't think I'll be participating in this part of the journey. In fact, I think I'll just head back."

"You're quitting?" Katherine sounded shocked.

"Not quitting, exactly. Just hedging my bets. I've never flown a hang glider before and I'm not sure right now is the time to begin."

Katherine took the glider that Haddi handed her and began to strap it on her back. She moved her backpack to the front for balance and adjusted the straps until they were comfortable.

"I'm sorry to hear that you're not going with us," she said. "It's really a lot of fun. The feelings you get when you're in the air are so spectacular. It's really worth overcoming the fear factor."

"What if I overcome the fear and still end up skewered on a sharp rock?"

"I guess that's possible, but it's never happened to anyone on any of the trips I've been on. If you listen to Haddi's instructions and have a little faith in yourself, it's really rather simple."

Melissa watched Elise, Richard and Mary strap on their kites, then held her hand out automatically to take the one that Haddi handed her.

"O friend, give up thy self that thou mayest find the Peerless One, pass by this mortal earth that thou mayest seek a home in the nest of heaven," Haddi said. "I cannot describe to you the beauty, the serenity of this journey. You must decide to embark upon it with your own free will. God brings forth His revelation, writes His laws upon the tablet of the heart, and shines His grace upon all His creatures equally. You have seen this with your own eyes, heard it with your own ears. But you must choose to follow. In that choosing, thou wilt loose thyself from all things else, and bind thyself to Him, and throw thy life down in His path, and cast thy soul away. There is God, and there is naught else beside Him."

Melissa felt tears rise and overflow her eyes, but she did not wipe them away. In the Valley of Search, she had given up her idea of finding her way before the path was made clear. In the Valley of Love, she had to sit near the burning fire to cleanse and purify her spirit, even though it was the exact opposite of what she desired.

In the Valley of Knowledge, she had passed through the Gate of Truth and Piety and faced her inner self, the one she usually tried to hide behind platitudes and selective ignorance. And, just outside the Valley of Unity, she had dreamed of floating above the earth, seeing the essential unity of all created things.

Now she was standing on the edge of a steep precipice, holding onto a kite of dubious construction and being asked to detach herself from life itself, if need be, to unite herself with her Creator.

What if the winds of contentment really would lift her high above the dangers below and carry her safely over the valley? Would the thrill be worth the risk?

She could see the cloud-covered slopes of Mount Eternity beckoning her. Did she really want to turn back now when she was so close? Could she trust God enough to put her whole life in His hands?

"Let us take a moment to pray and meditate on the flight ahead," Haddi suggested.

The group gathered and stood silently, allowing whatever supplications they chose to fill their minds and hearts. Melissa watched the others. They looked so serene, so confident, so willing. She felt so small and scared and insignificant.

"God will compensate each one out of His abundance," Haddi murmured. "He will turn sorrow to bliss, anguish to joy. Grief and mourning will yield to delight and rapture."

Melissa sighed, allowing her breath to escape slowly until she was empty. She reached deep down inside herself in search of a prayer. O God. I have come to know of you and love you on this journey. Each time I have felt down or sad or impatient, you have found a way to buoy me up. When I have strayed you have shown me the right path. Is flying over this valley like sitting by the fire of purification? I told you then that I am yours to do with as you will. Is this my test?

Melissa closed her eyes and let the winds of contentment blow around her. It felt as though the wind would lift her off the Plain of the Spirit and carry her into the sky, kite or no kite. The wind felt strong and she raised her arms, experimenting with its pull. Her hair whipped in disarray around her face and she felt her scalp tingle with the stimulation. The tingling increased until she felt the fingers of the wind caressing her whole body, pushing her, encouraging her.

She opened her eyes and sighed again. This time the wind took her sigh and propelled it across the valley. She imagined that she could watch it as it dipped and hovered and was carried safely across.

"All right. I'll go," she said, but she wasn't sure whether she had spoken it aloud or inside her head.

Haddi smiled, his eyes still closed.

A few moments later they were all strapped into their harnesses and ready to fly.

Melissa swallowed the lump in her throat and

concentrated on Haddi's instructions.

"Use your arms to keep your kite level. If you want to turn, just a slight movement of your hands on the steering bar will change your direction. I'll be right beside you to guide you into the air currents."

"I'm still scared," Melissa told Elise.

"Me too," she said, her eyes shining with anticipation. "But it's a good kind of scared. Just think of the stories I'll be able to tell my grandchildren."

If we live through it, Melissa thought, but immediately erased the negative image. We will make it. We will!

"On my signal, I want Katherine and Melissa to leap off the cliff first. Ten seconds later, Mary and Richard will go, then Elise and I will follow," Haddi instructed. "Ready?"

Melissa and Katherine nodded. "You'll love it!" Katherine whispered just before Haddi dropped his hand and told them to jump.

Melissa took one more deep breath to calm herself, then stopped thinking about the consequences and jumped.

"Whoooooaaaaa!" she yelled as the kite plunged straight down.

Beside her Katherine plummeted also.

The valley floor rushed up to greet them. Melissa could make out the crystal crusts on the jagged spires, could feel the spray of the turbulent waters. In a second, she knew that it would all be over.

Instead of her life flashing before her eyes, she saw the future she would never have.

Then a funny thing happened. Her mind instantly decided not to dwell on the past or her future death, but

to rejoice in the moment. Free falling was so fantastic, so exhilarating.

Beside her, Katherine smiled.

Melissa smiled back.

"Hold on!" Katherine shouted.

A second later, a huge current of warm air caught their kites and propelled them upward. In a rush which left Melissa gasping for breath, it lifted them clear of the spikes and the spray, high above the frothing waters to the vantage point of the birds.

'See, I told you it was simple.'

Melissa looked over at Katherine. She hadn't spoken but, nevertheless, Melissa had heard the words, almost as if they had appeared in her mind.

'I have no words to describe the feeling,' Melissa thought and in her mind, Katherine answered, 'I know.'

What was going on? Were they communicating mind to mind? Heart to heart? Telepathically?

Melissa didn't want to take the time to analyze it. There had been so many mysterious events on this journey that she had ceased wondering about them. For a moment she even contemplated the thought that this was yet another dream, or maybe still the same dream, and that she would wake up in her sleeping bag, next to the fire, back in the Valley of Knowledge.

She just wanted to drink in the beauty around her. She wanted to experience it with all of her senses as fully as possible because she knew that she would never be able to describe accurately the feeling of soaring, weightless, above the Valley of Contentment.

Suddenly she heard Master Eshgh's voice in her head. 'If I tried to speak of it, my tongue would tie in knots, and if I tried to write about it, the pen would leave only a blot.' Or was it her own thoughts?

'This mystery of inner meaning may be whispered only from heart to heart, confided only from breast to breast,' Katherine seemed to add.

It was as though she could hear the words without them ever being spoken. Every one of Melissa's senses felt finely tuned. Her sight was as sharp as an eagle's. She could see the tiniest grain of sand below and distinguish the drops of moisture in the clouds above. 'Truly, God is everywhere. The beauty of the Friend is in everything.'

Her kite carried her effortlessly, so that soon she was able to forget how scared she had been and only experience the joy. She grasped with lucid heart the subtle verities of creation, the total connectedness. The warmth of the air around her, the smells of the water below, the biting taste of the misty trailers from the clouds, the cry of sea birds, dipping and sailing beside her, all served to enhance the moment.

She had never felt so content in all her life. The world and everything in it, the universe and everything in it, were perfect. Her worries about school, her parents, her boyfriend, her future, were gone. Contentment, joy and rapture had replaced anxiety, grief and anguish. She was complete.

As she and Katherine sailed along, Haddi and the others caught up with them, until all six were floating in loose formation, riding the same crest of wind.

'We must go down,' Haddi communicated silently.

They all followed without question, guiding their kites almost as if by thought. Slowly they circled above the water. Down, down, without question, without hesitation, with no land in sight.

Melissa was sorry to have the flight end because she

had never felt so utterly at peace, but each valley had been better and more intriguing than the last, so she followed, because she knew she must. It was her destiny.

Before this trip her life had been trivial and unproductive, shrouded with veils, hiding her true self. But now, with piercing sight, she was able to gaze on creation in a new way, and she knew her life would never be the same.

'The Ocean of Grandeur,' Haddi communicated by thought as they neared the gently swelling waves. 'Drop out of your kites into the water.'

Melissa reached for the harness release and opened the buckle. A second later, she floated softly on the surface of the water.

CHAPTER 16

Melissa rejoiced in the refreshing coolness of the water. She bobbed along and found herself able to float effortlessly.

"Katherine," she called.

"Over here!" Katherine answered.

"What kind of water is this?" Melissa asked in wonderment. "I don't even have to tread water to stay afloat."

"This is the Ocean of Grandeur," Katherine told her. "The salt keeps you up."

"Amazing!" Elise said.

"Incredible," Richard added.

"I'm unsinkable!" Mary said, then giggled.

Haddi tilted backward as though in a watery rocking chair, his hands behind his head, his feet crossed at the ankles.

Melissa laughed. "Watch this!" she said, then spun in an effortless circle.

Katherine copied her move and they did an impromptu water ballet.

"Isn't it great? You never sink and you never get tired," Mary said. "I'm astonished, to say the least."

"Welcome to the Valley of Wonderment," Haddi

said.

"Ohhh! Ahhh!" Melissa couldn't stop exclaiming. The water was such a comfortable temperature – not too warm, not too cold. The waves were gentle swells, lifting her lightly, then drifting her back down. From water level, she had an exceptional view of the peaks which she had marveled at from the air. They were sandstone, polished smooth by the winds of contentment and worn to symmetrical perfection by the rolling waters.

"What do you think?" Katherine asked.

"It's . . . it's . . . " Melissa was struck dumb, completely unable to find the words to describe her feelings about the beauty of the All-Glorious Creator.

To say she was awed by the works of the Lord of Oneness was an understatement. Astonished, incredulous, amazed – all these words fell short of her growing wonder.

"I do know that I've been missing so much in my old life," Melissa said at last. "I'm beginning to see that wealth has nothing to do with money. A person can be wealthy of spirit in absolute poverty. And freedom, something I've always valued so deeply because I felt I had none, is only a state of mind."

"True freedom is freedom from ignorance and recognizing how impotent we are in the face of God's power," Katherine mused.

"That's so true," Melissa agreed. "The strongest shackles couldn't prevent me from reliving this moment and being free, no matter what my life circumstances are, because I could replay it over and over in my mind."

Katherine laughed. "For someone who didn't know what to say a moment ago, you just said an awful lot."

"I feel like I'm dreaming – first flying and now

floating around in an inland ocean only a few miles from my house that I didn't even know existed. The journey to Mount Eternity is like a wondrous, new creation, unparalleled in the known world."

"And yet, it's here all the time. All you have to do is want to make the trip."

"How can a valley be all water?" Richard asked.

"The Valley of Wonderment consists of the Ocean of Grandeur and the lower peaks of the Summits of Wonderment, yonder," Haddi told him. "We must swim there."

Melissa gazed across the azure waters to the distant mountains which were splashed with the oranges, golds and coppers of the setting sun. If she was having to struggle to swim, they would have seemed an improbable distance. Surely, in any other body of water, she wouldn't have been able to swim that far, but the Ocean of Grandeur gave her strength and the waves pushed her along toward her goal.

While they swam, Haddi spoke of the worlds of God.

"You mentioned that you felt as if this entire trip was like a beautiful dream," Haddi said, paddling along beside her. "Dreams are very insightful. You can witness a myriad perfect wisdoms and learn a myriad new and wondrous truths while dreaming. Behold how many secrets are deposited therein, how many wisdoms treasured up, how many worlds concealed.

"You might be asleep in your bed, or," he glanced meaningfully at Melissa, "in your sleeping bag on the open meadow, yet suddenly you find yourself in a far-off city, or far above the earth, without moving your feet or tiring your body; without using your eyes, you can see; without taxing your ears, you can hear; without a tongue, you can speak."

"That's happened to me before," Melissa said. "On this trip, even. While I was asleep in the Valley of Knowledge, I dreamed that a shining man bore me up on wings of light, high above the earth, and taught me the meaning of unity. Then, when we hiked up to the Schoolhouse of Oneness, Master Eshgh looked exactly like the shining man in my dream. Without the wings, of course."

"It is not uncommon to witness in the outer world, the very things you dream about," Haddi explained. "Some call it extrasensory perception, some call it vision, some call it premonition. The differences between the inner world, where without eye and ear and hand and tongue, a man puts all of these to use, and the outer world of physical reality, are difficult to comprehend. These two worlds conceal many mysteries."

Melissa paddled and thought, then turned on her back and thought some more. Finally she wondered aloud, "Perhaps God gives us dreams as glimpses of His different worlds. If, in a dream, you can exist and move about without your body, then we can imagine that death should be no barrier."

"Indeed," Haddi confirmed. "*God, the Exalted, hath placed these signs in men, to the end that philosophers may not deny the mysteries of the life beyond nor belittle that which hath been promised them.*"

"There are so many mysteries," Elise pondered. "Yet, in this Valley of Wonderment, I feel they are all explained."

"*Bind not thine heart to the earth; thou art a dweller in the court of nearness – choose not the homeland of the dust,*" Haddi exhorted.

"I've spent so much time by-passing the true meaning of my life, I haven't realized the connection between all of God's creatures, nor my place in the plan," Mary added.

The treasure at the end of the journey seems irrelevant now, Melissa thought. The lessons she had learned and the lessons she knew she was still to learn were really enough.

As she swam along, gradually closing the distance between herself and the Summits of Wonderment, she thought of all the bad things (or seemingly bad things) that had happened in her life. She thought of Dobson and his indifference to her wants and needs, to her goals and aspirations. She thought of her grandmother's death when she was only eight, and how sorrowfully she had grieved. She thought about how important the cheerleading squad had seemed when she tried out for it, and how devastated she had been when she didn't make it. She thought of working really hard to win at a track meet, then stumbling at the last moment, her opponent passing her at the finish line.

In God's overall plan, those things didn't mean very much. And she would always be connected to her grandmother because death was only an illusion, another gate to pass through on the path toward God.

"Nothing can befall me, but what God has destined," Melissa said aloud, "and every test makes me stronger and more able to take on the next test. In fact, I'm actually looking forward to more tests and growing pains."

"A week ago I would have found that hard to believe," Elise said. "But I'm feeling the same way. Bring on the toughest trail, the highest mountain, the widest desert, the most untamed river. I'm ready!"

"Not me," Richard grimaced. "I'm ready for a rest."

Everyone laughed, and as they were laughing a large swell rose up behind them and propelled them onward in a rush of froth and foam toward the beach. A second later, Melissa's feet touched sand, and she stood up, ready to take on the Summits of Wonderment.

"Let's rest here for the night and dry out our packs," Haddi suggested. "That way we will be fresh for the final leg of our journey tomorrow. We'll want to start before daybreak."

Richard groaned. "Going back to the City of Love is looking better and better."

That night Melissa dreamed no dreams. Dark and velvet, the soft night enveloped her until she awoke the following morning to the melodious sound of Haddi chanting a dawn prayer.

After a breakfast of tea and oatmeal, Haddi gathered the group in a circle.

"We have been through much together," he said. "Each of us has learned about ourselves and our capabilities. Nothing that we have learned will be lost unless we wish it so."

"You sound as if you're about to leave us," Richard said.

"I will always be with you in spirit," Haddi told them. "But now there is a choice for you to make, and you must make it alone."

Melissa shivered, despite the fact that her clothes were fully dry. Somehow she knew that every lesson she had learned on this trip had all led up to this moment. Behind her, the softly lapping waters of the Ocean of Grandeur caressed the sand. In front of her, a scant half-mile from the sandy beach where they stood, the lofty range of the Summits of Wonderment rose explosively toward the sky. Beyond them, the highest peak, Mount Eternity, shot upward, towering over the Summits like a father over his children.

"There are two paths to choose from at this point," Haddi continued. "Both take you through the Summits of Wonderment. You can see Mount Eternity in the distance, there." He pointed toward the east, where predawn, heavy and gray, cloaked the splendid mountain.

"Which one do we take?" Mary asked. "Will both lead to Mount Eternity?"

"Eventually, every path leads to Mount Eternity," Haddi assured her. He waved his arm to indicate the two signposts before them. "This one," he said, pointing to the one on the left, "heads out over the flats and through the mountains by way of that pass over there."

Melissa looked at the path. It looked easy. The way was surprisingly flat and meandered over first the beach and then the low foothills before slipping through a wide pass in the Summits of Wonderment and heading off in the direction of Mount Eternity. Mount Eternity was clearly visible through the crack in the mountains and the path seemed to aim directly toward it over gently rolling terrain. There was plenty of water along the way as a stream flowed beside the trail.

"The other path," Haddi continued, "goes over the Summits of Wonderment."

Melissa turned her head and tried to follow with her eyes the path that seemed to meander around in purposeless zigzags up the side of the Summits of Wonderment, by the most difficult route possible.

"What's the difference?" Melissa asked. "Except that

one looks harder and the other easier?"

"The difference is that, though both appear to lead directly to Mount Eternity, this is only an illusion. One leads directly back to the Valley of Search, where the wayfarer must start over, seeking the correct choices and the right path," Haddi said.

"Well, I've made my choice," Richard announced. "I'm going to take the path on the left. That way I can keep Mount Eternity in sight and not get lost traipsing around on the side of another mountain."

Haddi nodded. He reached out to shake Richard's hand. "May you find the treasure of inestimable value on your way."

"Thank you. This has been a terrific trip. I'm really glad we came. And, if we end up in the Valley of Search again, that's not a problem, because Mary and I have talked about it and we really would like to get another look at the City of Love."

Mary hesitated only a second, then joined her husband at the trail head. "We appreciate all you've done for us, Haddi," she said. "Maybe if we end up living in the City of Love, we'll see you again on one of your journeys."

"May God shine His light upon you," Haddi replied. "I'm sure we'll meet again."

Elise smiled, tightened the straps on her backpack, and started off on the path to the right. "See you at Mount Eternity," she said.

Melissa didn't know what to do. She looked from Haddi to Katherine and back again, searching for a clue in their faces. "Which path do you think we should take?" she finally asked Katherine. "You've been on this journey before. You must know the right way."

"Every time we come on the journey we cross the mountains at a different spot. The journey changes with the people who take it. I wish I could tell you, but I don't know the way myself."

Melissa stood up straighter and looked after Richard and Mary as they hiked steadily along the flatland trail. Then she watched Elise's retreating back as she started her slow climb to the base of the Summits of Wonderment.

She closed her eyes and said a silent prayer of praise and gratitude to God for giving her this test.

"I think I'll take the path over the mountains," Melissa said when she opened her eyes.

"Why is that?" Katherine asked.

"Because nothing else has come easily on this journey, why should this? I look at that mountain trail and the first thing that comes to mind is growth instead of speed. I'll bet there are a few tests and difficulties along that jagged path that I still need to overcome, a few lessons I still need to learn."

Melissa put one foot on the path and touched the signpost gingerly. The words read, '*O Lord, increase my astonishment at Thee.*' Then she stepped out on her own, her eyes fixed on the steep and rocky trail before her.

A second later, Katherine joined her. "We may as well finish this together," she said, "one way or the other."

CHAPTER 17

Melissa almost changed her mind when she reached the foot of the mountain. Elise, although she had only struck out moments before them, was already swallowed up in the heavy mist which robed the mountain.

"This path looks harder than I thought," Melissa said, looking up into the shrouds of mist. "I wish the sun would come out so that the Summits of Wonderment wouldn't look so dreary."

"Do you want to turn back and take the other path?" Katherine asked.

Melissa straightened her shoulders and felt the weight of the backpack's straps bite into her shoulders. Her clothes were stiff from the salt water and rough against her skin. "No," she declared, "we can do this. We're good hikers. We've come this far and God won't put a test before us that we can't overcome."

"You sound awfully sure of yourself," Katherine remarked, peering up the side of the mountain into the mist. "The other path looks easier, and straighter."

"You're not giving up on me, are you?" Melissa asked.

"No way!" Katherine said. "I just wanted to make sure that you knew what you were doing."

"Maybe I didn't before I came on this trip, but I do

now! I'm going to scale this mountain and conquer Mount Eternity. There's no turning back now. It's only onward and upward!"

Melissa put her foot on the upslope and started climbing. Her boots scraped against her socks which, in turn, chafed her tender feet. With each step she felt the weight of her backpack more acutely. She wished she could just take it off and cast it away, but what would she do for food, for clothing, for shelter? After all, to get home once they reached Mount Eternity, they had to hike back to the Valley of Search.

The higher they went the more tired and winded she became. The path did just as she expected. It twisted and turned and crawled up the side of the Summits of Wonderment with agonizing slowness.

"It's only been fifteen minutes, and it seems like hours," Melissa said.

Katherine peered back down in the direction they had come. "I can't even see the Ocean of Grandeur any more. The mist covers everything."

"Where's the path up ahead?" No matter how hard Melissa tried, all she saw were mist-shrouded boulders and brush.

"I don't know," Katherine said, peering into the fog. "I can't see a thing."

"I feel wetter now than I felt when we were swimming in the water yesterday," Melissa added as she adjusted her soggy, fog-soaked pack and wiggled her damp toes in her socks. "Here, I thought I was going to storm straight over the Summits of Wonderment to Mount Eternity and conquer it, and now I'm afraid that final peak is going to conquer me."

"No it won't. All we have to do is keep climbing. If

we're going up, we'll be going in the right direction," Katherine told her. "C'mon, we're in this together. You said so yourself."

Melissa smiled. "I was so proud of myself for getting this far. I had already begun to think about what I was going to say to Dobson and my parents when I returned. It seems that as soon as I started patting myself on the back for the great job I was doing, the path became harder."

"Pride won't get us up this mountain, that's for sure," Katherine remarked.

"How about a burro named Humility?" Melissa asked, only half joking.

"I think we're on our own. Besides, it can't get much worse, can it?"

And then it started to rain.

"Is it my imagination, or is the mist getting heavier?" Katherine commented.

Melissa held out her hand. "Definitely dripping. Just what we need, a storm. We'd better get a move on."

The girls began climbing again. All day Melissa just concentrated on putting one foot in front of the other. Each time she stumbled, she picked herself up. Her hands were scraped and bleeding from trying to hold onto the slippery rocks to pull herself up the steep mountainside. There was no longer any vestige of a path, no goal in sight, no beginning to judge their progress. There was only one rock at a time and the sound of the rain and wind.

Lightning cracked, illuminating the eerie landscape.

"Maybe we should stop and rest until the storm blows over?" Katherine called over the whine of the wind.

"It might not blow over for a while and it won't be

long before it starts getting dark," Melissa called back, the gusts grabbing at her voice. "I guess we should find some shelter."

Lightning split the sky again as if in response.

She looked up during the brief flash, trying to make out shapes in the mist ahead. She thought she saw an overhang of rock, but she couldn't be sure until she got closer.

Melissa leaned close to Katherine. "Let's try up there to the left," she suggested. "It's almost straight up, but I think we can make it."

Katherine nodded and painstakingly they began to climb the last few feet to shelter and safety.

The overhang turned out to be a cave of sorts and Melissa hurried to reach the dry interior. Only a small ledge was left between them and sanctuary.

Suddenly her foot slipped out from under her and she went down, grabbing for the ledge as she went.

"Aaaah!"

Her fingers slipped and slid on the smooth stone, finally finding a grip on the edge itself. But her feet were dangling in midair and her backpack hung askew, its weight dragging her, pulling her downward.

"Hold on!" Katherine cried, lying flat on the path and reaching out to her. "Grab my hand!"

Melissa gripped her friend's hand and tried to pull herself up, but she couldn't do it. "How far is down?" she gasped as she let go of Katherine's hand and felt for a good hold on the rocky ledge. "What if I fall?"

"I don't know," Katherine quickly replied. "I can't see the bottom. You look like you're hanging off into space. Drop the backpack!"

"I can't. The food! My stuff! Besides, I can't hold on

with one hand!"

"Try to pull yourself up again."

"I'm too heavy and my arms are too weak."

"Wait! Let me see if I have some rope," Katherine said, throwing her pack on the ground and rummaging through it.

Melissa closed her eyes and concentrated on her fingertips. I'll hold on to the count of twenty-five, she thought. Then she counted, slowly. Now I'll hold on to the count of fifteen.

Her backpack felt like a lead weight. If she let go of it, she would lose all that she came with. Everything that she had brought with her from her old life. But did she really need those things? Look how much she had gained. And what good would they do her if she were dead?

"Cut the straps!" Melissa yelled.

Katherine was there immediately, sawing at the straps with her pocket knife, grabbing for Melissa's wrist as the shift in weight pulled her off balance.

"C'mon. You can do it!" she yelled. "Give it all you've got!"

Melissa pulled her leg up, trying to swing it onto the ledge, trying to find a foothold. Her fingertips were numb. The wind and the rain and the storm seemed distant. The only thing she could feel was Katherine's hand, gripping her wrist.

Then, without conscious thought, she stopped struggling. "God," she said. "I have given my will over to you. My fate is in your hands. Give me the strength or let me fall. My life is yours either way."

A sudden tingle of energy charged through her. She took a deep breath and heaved with all of her might. In an instant, she pulled herself up and over the ledge. A second later, she and Katherine were both lying, panting, on the floor of the cave. Exhausted, they fell asleep where they lay.

"What happened last night, when you suddenly flung yourself up onto the ledge?" Katherine asked when they awoke a few hours later.

"I stopped trying so hard to save myself and allowed God's will to prevail," Melissa told her. "In that final instant before I pulled myself up, I realized that all of my earthly possessions didn't matter. It doesn't matter if I grow up to be dirt poor and live in the dust. What does matter is richness in God."

"You could have died back there!" Katherine said.

"I'm not afraid to die any more," Melissa told her truthfully. "I know that death is just part of the process. That's what Master Eshgh meant when he said that all of the signs were there so that we couldn't disbelieve in life after death. When I stopped struggling, I felt only peace."

"Wow!"

"I know, wow! This sure isn't what I expected to learn on this trip," Melissa said.

Katherine smiled. "I learn something new every time I come, too. I guess that's because God is infinite, and we can never learn all there is to know in one lifetime, maybe not even in eternity."

"Is that the sun?" Melissa exclaimed, leaning past Katherine to look outside. "I don't believe it! The storm is over and the sun is beginning to rise!"

Katherine turned to look.

Sure enough, predawn light poured into the opening of their little cave and illumined the damp floor, turning it silver. Outside, every puddle, every tree, every rock and every flower shimmered.

"There are flowers!" Melissa cried.

"And trees!" Katherine shouted.

"Why didn't we see them before? Were they here all along?"

Katherine shrugged her shoulders. "And look!" she said, pointing to their right. "We're almost at the top!"

The girls crawled out of the cave and stood up. They looked out over a meadow dotted with shining puddles and flower-laden trees. Each pool and puddle shone with pearls and precious stones, and gems of inestimable value were strewn about the landscape.

But Melissa didn't pause to gather the stones or pick the flowers. She wasn't even tempted. All she wanted to do was gaze on the face of Mount Eternity at sunrise.

"Everything is coming alive," Melissa said, shielding her eyes from the sudden glare as they walked over a small hill and beheld the snow-capped peak, their goal and desire, Mount Eternity.

From behind the majestic peak, the sun shot forth its welcome rays in the most beautiful sunrise she had ever seen. Every glorious color of the rainbow brushed the eastern sky. Clouds parted, leaving dawn-shaded trails.

"God is rising out of the darkness on the horizon of Eternity," Melissa added in a whisper, then dropped silently to her knees in the soft moss to absorb the moment.

"Our transformation is only possible through God's will," Katherine said.

"I feel so close to God here, as if I can almost touch Him," Melissa commented. She was surprised to hear herself say that, but it was true. It was as if she gave up her will back on the ledge in the storm. When she abandoned thoughts of herself and her life as she knew it, she gained the universe.

She took a deep breath and stood up, ready to go through the last valley, the Valley of Poverty and Absolute Nothingness, to reach her fondest desire.

Suddenly it seemed that there were people everywhere. One moment they had knelt, alone, on the Summits of Wonderment, and the next they saw dozens of people climbing up the opposite side of the hill carrying pouches and bags. The people grabbed at the diamonds and emeralds and stuffed them into their packs.

"Who are these people?" Melissa asked.

"They are the glory-seekers, the gold diggers," Katherine said.

"This is the treasure, isn't it?" Melissa remarked.

Katherine looked around at the gems and gold beneath their feet.

"No, not the jewels," Melissa answered herself. "Nearness to God."

"It's true. The heedless come every day and grab for their fortunes. But when the jewels are disturbed, they turn to tinsel and base metal. But they still come back the next day, hoping that it will be different."

"We should tell them, give them a clue, so that they don't spend their lives in fruitless searching."

"The heedless haven't even reached the Valley of Search. And everyone *must* search," Katherine said. "Some in the Valley of Search, some on the Summits of Wonderment, others by the Sea of Spirit."

"I still wish I could help them. Excuse me," Melissa said, tapping a woman on the shoulder. "These jewels aren't the treasure. Nearness to God is the treasure. And likeness to God is the means of attaining it. Put back the diamonds and come with us to Mount Eternity."

The woman simply shook her head and reached for another stone.

"Won't you look beyond your greed and see that God is near?" Melissa asked another.

"You're standing on my emeralds," the man said, ignoring her words.

"You must adorn yourself with God's attributes, not worthless jewels," Katherine said.

"Maybe they're worthless to you, but not to me," the man said. "God says we must strive for perfection," he added boastfully. "Well, I'm striving to find the most perfect emerald!"

"I don't think –" Melissa began.

"That's the problem," the woman said, cutting her off. "Young people these days don't think! I'm going to build a huge temple to God when I cash in my jewels. Then God will reward me for being His true servant."

She went back to digging in the dirt.

Melissa shook her head. "Why is it so hard to make them see?"

"We can never *make* them see, Melissa. I guess they'll understand when they're ready," Katherine said.

Melissa looked toward Mount Eternity. "I think it's time for us to go on," she said.

In front of them the path reappeared and straightened out. It was easy to follow now so Katherine and Melissa walked past the treasure-seekers who were so caught up in their folly.

"I still want to teach them," Melissa said. "I want to tell them what I've learned."

"Don't worry, you will," Katherine said. "There will

be lots of chances to teach."

The path led them through a copse of trees and curved downward slightly. They had reached the other side of the mountain range and looked out over a sea of mist beneath which nothing was visible.

And, in front of them on the path, waiting patiently on a wooden bench, sat Haddi.

CHAPTER 18

"Haddi!" Melissa called, waving as she ran to greet him. "How did you . . . ? Never mind. I've learned to accept the unexplainable."

Haddi chuckled. "Then it really *has* been quite a journey!"

"Hi, Haddi!" Katherine said, jogging up beside Melissa. "That was quite a climb! Where's Elise?"

"She has already gone on to Mount Eternity," Haddi said. "She is quite a remarkable woman. I'm sure God is pleased."

Melissa looked out over the blanket of mist which completely obliterated any view of the Valley of Poverty and Absolute Nothingness. She could clearly see the Summits of Wonderment where they stood, and the top of Mount Eternity, now glowing in the morning sun. But the valley between was hidden, blank, the embodiment of its name because she could see absolutely nothing of it, and it was completely devoid of the riches apparent on the Summits of Wonderment. The path they had been following led straight to the edge and then disappeared.

"How did she get there?" Melissa asked. "I don't see any way across. Did she fly? Hike down into the mist? Swim? We're ready for anything so long as it brings us nearer to God."

Haddi laughed again. He reached up into the Tree of Truth and plucked two ripe fruits. He offered them to Katherine and Melissa. "You found the treasure, then?"

"The treasure is knowing and loving God, nearness to Him and detachment from the world," Melissa said without hesitation. She took a bite of the succulent peach, and let its warm juice run down her chin. "God always provides," she added.

"What is the secret of the path?" Haddi asked.

Melissa thought for a few moments while she finished her peach. Katherine stood, silently, supporting her. Melissa knew that this was the time to put into words all that she had learned. As she let her gaze drift to the uppermost pinnacle of Mount Eternity her confidence grew.

"One must not stray from the law," Melissa began. "That's the secret of the path.

"In the Valley of Search, I learned that it was the quality of my search that counted. I found that without patience I can't attain any goals. In the Valley of Love I realized that one must cling to the robe of obedience and shun all forbidden things. I have to submit my will to God's. In the Valley of Knowledge I began to see beauty and joy in all things, happiness in hardship, death in life, the end in the beginning. I found that everything is part of the process."

"And in the Valley of Unity?" Haddi prompted.

Melissa sighed in remembrance. "My dream led me from the Valley of Knowledge into the Valley of Unity. From the heights of glory I realized that every creature belongs to God equally. His love shines on all, His Faith encompasses all without prejudice or barriers, without name or fame or rank to interfere. Flying over the Valley of Contentment, I took stock of my life and realized how much I've been missing by denying my spiritual nature. When we plunged into the Ocean of Grandeur in the Valley of Wonderment, I knew that anything was possible if God wills it and I put my heart and soul into it."

Melissa picked another peach and savored its tangy sweetness. "Climbing up the Summits of Wonderment was the biggest lesson," she declared. "I had to let go of everything I held dear. I even had to accept death before God gave me the strength to save myself. None of the jewels or treasures matter. There is only God."

"It's time to cross," Haddi announced.

Melissa stared at the sight before her. While she had been talking, the mist had drawn away and revealed a long rope bridge spanning the chasm over the Valley of True Poverty and Absolute Nothingness. It led directly to the side of Mount Eternity where she could clearly make out a set of steps up to the top.

The three travelers stepped onto the gently swaying bridge and started across, leaving the summit meadow and all of the treasure-seekers behind.

"Why don't the other people take the bridge across to Mount Eternity?" Melissa asked.

"The way is veiled to them by the light," Haddi explained.

"Yet the light shows us the way," Katherine added.

Melissa peered over the edge of the bridge, but the valley floor wasn't visible. She could almost believe that there really was nothing but mist below them – absolute nothingness.

She wasn't afraid. She was exhilarated. She had

nothing left but, in exchange, she had everything.

There were signs posted along the way.

"*Only through obedience to the laws of God, as revealed by His Messengers, can one attain unto the Divine Presence,*" Melissa read aloud.

"*This is the changeless Faith of God, eternal in the past, eternal in the future,*" Katherine quoted.

"*He is the first and the last; the Seen and the Hidden; and He knoweth all things,*" Haddi said.

With each step they took, the signs poured forth the wisdom of the Manifestations of God.

"*The tabernacle of unity hath been raised; regard ye not one another as strangers.*"

"*Let your vision be world-embracing, rather than confined to your own self.*"

"*The Lord our God is one Lord.*"

"*He is God, the one and Only; God the Eternal, Absolute . . . and there is none like unto Him.*"

"*There is no likeness of Him whose glory is infinite.*"

"*Behold the universe in the glory of God, and all that lives and moves on earth.*"

When they reached the far side of the bridge, Melissa took the steps two at a time. Her heart soared and her feet had wings. Inscriptions were carved into each stair riser.

"*This station is the dying from self and the living in God, the being poor in self and rich in the Desired One.*"

"*O my friend, listen with heart and soul to the songs of the spirit, and treasure them as thine own eyes.*"

"*Make thou an effort, that haply in this dust-heap of the mortal world thou mayest catch a fragrance from the everlasting garden.*"

"*Now hast thou abandoned the drop of life and come to*

the sea of the Life-Bestower."

"Free thyself from that which thy passion desireth; then advance unto thy Lord."

Melissa reached the top and stopped, awe-struck.

Before her stood an ethereal temple, nine-sided, drawing in the light from the sun and reflecting it in all directions. She realized immediately that it was this same light that had bathed her when she stood in front of her house, trying to decide whether to come on this trip or not.

Without another moment's hesitation, she stepped within the temple and raised her voice in prayer.

"All praise, O my God, be to Thee Who art the Source of all glory and majesty, of greatness and honor, of sovereignty and dominion, of loftiness and grace, of awe and power. Whomsoever Thou willest Thou causest to draw nigh unto the Most Great Ocean, and on whomsoever Thou desirest Thou conferrest the honor of recognizing Thy Most Ancient Name. Of all who are in heaven and on earth, none can withstand the operation of Thy sovereign Will. From all eternity Thou didst rule the entire creation, and Thou wilt continue for evermore to exercise Thy dominion over all created things. There is none other God but Thee, the Almighty, the Most Exalted, the All-Powerful, the All-Wise.

"Illumine, O Lord, the faces of Thy servants, that they may behold Thee; and cleanse their hearts that they may turn unto the court of Thy heavenly favors, and recognize Him who is the Manifestation of Thy Self and the Dayspring of Thine Essence. Verily, Thou art the Lord of all worlds. There is no God but Thee, the Unconstrained, the All-Subduing."

After her prayer, Melissa fell silent for a long time, meditating, contemplating, breathing in the ecstacy of knowing that she had attained the presence of God.

Knowing that, no matter how far away from this temple or Mount Eternity she ventured in her life, God would always be with her, in her.

Beside her she could hear Katherine and Haddi praying. She could feel their presence, but she was so tuned in to her own connection with God that they only added to her joy. She heard them leave, but she stayed where she was, drinking deeply of the living waters, allowing her soul to be quickened.

She finally opened her eyes, rose from where she had prostrated herself, and walked outside the temple to join Haddi and Katherine.

She stared out over the seven valleys, back to where they had started from. The mist made it impossible to see the exact route they would have to take on their journey back, but Melissa was actually looking forward to the trip.

"I'm ready to return now," she said, her face radiant with acquiescence.

Katherine took her hand and drew her to an ornate staircase behind the temple. There were seven steps leading down into a wall of mist.

By this time Melissa was accustomed to mist and she followed Katherine willingly down the small flight of stairs. At the bottom she turned and waved to Haddi, then stepped through the white curtain.

Surprise isn't a strong enough word for what she felt at the moment she emerged from the mist.

"I can't believe it!" Melissa cried. "We're right back where we started, in the meadow outside the Valley of Search!"

"It's not so difficult to understand, really," Katherine said, smiling. "The wayfarer can take seven thousand years to cross the seven valleys, or seven thousand days, or seven thousand hours . . . "

"Or seven days, or seven steps," Melissa added, picking up on Katherine's train of thought. "Or seven breaths."

"Or one breath, if God wills and desires it," Katherine concluded.

Melissa looked back at the wall of mist and sighed. She already missed being on the journey and felt her world crashing in on her.

"What's wrong?" Katherine asked.

"I just worry that I won't be able to keep my new perspective when I return to my old life. There are so many pressures, so many tests . . . "

"So many joys, so many challenges," Katherine reminded her. "So many others to teach and to invite on the journey to Mount Eternity, just as I did with you."

"You mean, I can go back to Mount Eternity any time I want to?" Melissa asked.

"In fact," Katherine replied as she gave Melissa a warm hug, "you're always there."